PENGUIN BOOKS

Finding the Heart Sutra

Alex Kerr is an American writer and Japanologist whose previous books include *Lost Japan* and *Another Kyoto*. He was the first foreigner to be awarded the Shincho Gakugei Literature Prize for the best work of non-fiction published in Japan.

T0002811

Finding the Heart Sutra

Guided by a Magician,
an Art Collector and Buddhist Sages
from Tibet to Japan

ALEX KERR

PENGUIN BOOKS

PENGUIN BOOKS

UK | USA | Canada | Ireland | Australia
India | New Zealand | South Africa

Penguin Books is part of the Penguin Random House group of companies
whose addresses can be found at global.penguinrandomhouse.com.

First published in Great Britain by Allen Lane 2021
Published in Penguin Books 2022
001

Printed and bound in Great Britain by Clays Ltd, Elcograf S.p.A.

The authorized representative in the EEA is Penguin Random House Ireland,
Morrison Chambers, 32 Nassau Street, Dublin D02 YH68

A CIP catalogue record for this book is available from the British Library

ISBN: 978-0-141-99420-8

www.greenpenguin.co.uk

MIX
Paper from
responsible sources
FSC® C018179

Penguin Random House is committed to a
sustainable future for our business, our readers
and our planet. This book is made from Forest
Stewardship Council® certified paper.

Contents

List of Calligraphies

Preface

Buddhist lore tells the story of a young seeker after wisdom who, after many adventures, climbs to the top of the Tower of Maitreya. To his disappointment, he finds there just one small room. But when he pushes open the door, inside is revealed a vast interior, a delirious vision of gleaming halls adorned with shining gems and crowned with radiant pinnacles bathed in showers of gold dust. Beyond that stretch other halls, an infinity of them, each more glorious than the last, all reflecting each other, yet all contained within Maitreya's Tower.

The Heart Sutra is such a room. Consisting of less than sixty lines, this brief poem on emptiness reveals itself to be the storehouse of a universe of thought.

Since I first learned about the Heart Sutra forty years ago, I have come to see it as one of the most thought-provoking and emotionally intense works produced by humankind. Measured by its influence across Asia since the seventh century – from Japan, Korea and China, to India, Mongolia, Tibet and Vietnam – no other work today comes close to the popularity of the Heart Sutra.

It is believed to contain the condensed essence of all Buddhist wisdom. Yet despite this, the Heart Sutra remains barely known in the West, even though it rivals the teachings of Laozi and Confucius in importance. Examine any word in the text and out spills a shower of gems, concepts that have inspired thinkers in East Asia for over thirteen hundred years.

Those thinkers range from the Chinese magician-philosopher Fazang in the seventh/eighth century to the sharp-tongued Japanese Zen master Hakuin in the eighteenth and, in our time, the Dalai Lama and the Vietnamese spiritual leader Thich Nhat Hanh. Augmenting these are many books and articles in English, Japanese and other languages published in modern times, as well as hundreds of internet sites and blogs about specialist aspects. Together these make up a vibrant international community, linked over continents and time.

In the interest of full disclosure, I must admit that I am not a monk, and nor am I a Buddhist scholar. That makes me poorly equipped for taking up a topic as monumental as the Heart Sutra. In my defence, I plead sheer length of time spent with this text – decades of involvement since I was very young. Even great masters of Buddhism have felt humbled when they tried to explain the Heart Sutra. The Mongolian lama Dendarla Rampa, on completing his commentary *Jewel Light Illuminating the Meaning of the Heart Sutra* around the year 1800, expressed a similar sense of inadequacy, imploring the reader to be understanding:

Like the barley collected by a beggar,
This is a mixture into one of a variety of texts.
It is not filled with profound statements.
But because it was done with a mind not black,
I don't think I am to be blamed.

Introduction

First Encounter

It was a hot July day in Kobe in 1978, and we had gathered to watch a world collapse. My mentor, art collector David Kidd, lived in the eighteenth-century palace of a Japanese feudal lord, which had been moved around 1900 from the grounds of a castle on the island of Shikoku to Ashiya, near Kobe. Since then, every other palace of its type had been destroyed, and this was the only one that was still lived in. Filled with David's incomparable collection of Japanese ink paintings, Chinese furniture and golden Tibetan Buddhas, the house was a precious survival of something long lost in China and Japan.

But the palace's time was up. The landlord had sold the plot on which it stood to a developer to build apartments. David had decided to dismantle the palace, as is often done with old wooden buildings in Japan, by removing the plaster walls and taking apart the columns and beams, which are fitted together without nails, like a giant balsa-wood puzzle. The structure can then be moved and reassembled in a new location. David planned to store the pieces of the palace in a warehouse, where they would lie until someone could raise the money to put them back together again.

I joined a group of David's friends who had assembled to bid farewell to the palace's silver-leafed doors and wide-columned halls. We each took a symbolic swing with a big wooden mallet to break down the earthen walls before the carpenters arrived to take apart the rest of building. Then off we drove to the Miyako Hotel in Kyoto where David had booked rooms to live in until he found a new home.

As we sat in David's hotel suite sipping restorative gin and tonics, the mood was glum. We all knew that this was the end of an era and we would never see anything like this in Japan again. Suddenly Urata, a high-spirited Zen monk from Kyoto, whipped out his blue-and-gold fan and begin whirling around the room. He was laughing, and in between bouts of laughter, he was chanting something, over and over again, in a thunderous voice. It was the Heart Sutra.

Kabuki

Years passed. The pieces of the palace were transferred from one storehouse to another until finally they disappeared. Nobody knows what happened to the columns and silver doors.

Meanwhile, I moved on. I became interested in kabuki. Smitten by the talent of Tamasaburo, kabuki's leading *onnagata* (male player of female roles), I went to see every play he appeared in, including *Dojoji*. It's about a dancing girl who gains entrance to a forbidden temple precinct, but once inside reveals herself as the spirit of a wrathful serpent. At the opening of the play, the girl engages in a Zen-style debate with a group of monks who are trying to bar her entry.

In the end she stumps them, quoting the core lines of the Heart Sutra. Everyone watching in the audience knew the words by heart: *Shiki soku ze ku, ku soku ze shiki* ('The material world is itself emptiness. Emptiness is itself the material world'). Beaten in the debate, the monks allow her into the temple grounds, to their later great regret when the spirit-serpent wraps itself around the temple's great bronze bell and melts it with its scorching body heat.

That was my second encounter with the Heart Sutra. In my ensuing decades in Japan, I came across it repeatedly, as it seeped into every part of the culture. Politicians quoted it; shops printed it as a design on fans, handbags and neckties.

Marguerite Yourcenar's Fan

One day sometime in the early 1980s, Tamasaburo, who had by then become a friend, asked me to come round to his back-stage room at the Kabukiza Theatre in Tokyo to interpret for a visitor from France. She was an elderly writer who was fascinated by the cult of evanescence in Japan – the idea that all things exist just for a precious moment, like cherry blossom petals that bloom only for a week and then scatter in the wind – and wanted to ask Tamasaburo some questions about kabuki. Entering the room, my heart skipped a beat as I realized that this was no ordinary visitor but the renowned French author Marguerite Yourcenar.

When I was a teenager, I used to go up into the dusty attic in our house in Alexandria, Virginia, to read books that my parents had stored there, and one of them was Yourcenar's grand historical novel *Memoirs of Hadrian* about the Roman emperor Hadrian. In real life, she turned out to be even grander than I had imagined. Swathed in what looked like layers of grey rags, her craggy figure towered over us like an imperious Rodin bronze.

Later Yourcenar came to Kyoto, where I was living, and we struck up a friendship. I would take her to my favourite temples, and she in turn told me stories about Emperor Hadrian and the Académie Française. One day we were walking through Kyoto and I found a fan inscribed with the Heart Sutra in gold on a blue background, like the one that Zen monk Urata had waved around at the Miyako Hotel. I bought it and gave it to her, and she tucked it away among her trademark great swag of grey draperies.

Yourcenar was intrigued. She was drawn to the philosophy behind the sutra, but she was also curious about the delicate calligraphy on the fan. That led me to talk with her about calligraphy, which has been a passion since I was first introduced to Chinese characters in primary school at the age of nine. Eventually Yourcenar suggested that we do a book together about the Heart Sutra: I would brush calligraphy for it, and she would write. But it never happened. She returned to France, and not long afterwards I heard she had died. They told me

that the object she kept with her until the very end was the fan inscribed with the Heart Sutra.

That was 1987. Over thirty years have passed since then, and now the time has come to finally write the book. But without Yourcenar, I have to do the writing myself.

The Sutras of Perfection of Wisdom

A sutra is a Buddhist scripture. Emphasis should be on the word 'a'. Hundreds of sutras exist, some long and some short, and from different periods, some appearing long after the death of the historical Buddha. Arising first in India, they travelled outwards to Tibet, China, Thailand and beyond, to what became the Buddhist world.

The Heart Sutra belongs to a category known as the Perfection of Wisdom sutras. At least three versions of this category of sutra exist, with 100,000 lines being considered 'long', 25,000 lines 'medium' and 8,000 lines 'short'.

In India, where the sutras come from, brevity had never been the soul of wit. The earliest works, believed to have been spoken by Buddha Shakyamuni himself in the sixth to fifth century BC and then transcribed in Sanskrit, are conveyed in a clear-cut, direct language. But by the time the later sutras came to be written down, they had acquired added colour, repetition and more detail, until Buddha's stark meditation mat had metamorphosed into a soaring Gothic cathedral. Over the centuries, the words piled up higher and higher into magnificent vaults and spires.

The Heart Sutra cuts through all of that. It's a digest, a drastic abridgement. Consisting of only 272 characters, it can be organized into fifty or sixty lines, depending on where phrases are cut – just the right length for fans and neckties. It has been revered since the time it first appeared as containing the essence of Buddhist wisdom.

We don't really know how it came into being. In some cloudy way in the seventh century A D, the sutra fell into the hands of Xuanzang, the monk who travelled from Chang'an, the capital of Tang dynasty China, to India in search of Buddhist scriptures, as recounted in the classic Chinese novel *Journey to the West*. After sixteen years in India, he returned to Chang'an in 645 with hundreds of scrolls, among which was the Heart Sutra.

Xuanzang devoted the later part of his life to translating into Chinese the entire Perfection of Wisdom corpus, including the full texts of the 'long', 'medium' and 'short' versions. In the process, he also translated the Heart Sutra, and he and his disciple Kuiji wrote the first commentaries. Other translators followed. Almost immediately the sutra gained wide popularity, and by the eighth century it had spread throughout the Buddhist world. Today, millions of people recite it daily, from Japan to Korea and Mongolia, down through China to Vietnam, and across to Tibet and India.

The Heart Sutra appeals at a deep emotional level like no other Buddhist writing. As to why this should be, a big part of its charm lies in the language. With other sutras you feel you're listening to a lecture by a pedantic professor; with the Heart Sutra you're hearing mischievously clever remarks from someone very wise. The style is concise and the phrasing elegant.

The repetitious cadence haunts the brain like the words to an old song.

The content of the sutra – the emptiness of life – is deep to the point of darkness, and therein lies its intense appeal. Strong tentacles reach out from this text, gripping us and pulling us into its black impenetrable waters. It's cool and quiet down there. The emptiness is irresistible.

The sutra is about achieving wisdom, but this wisdom is a little boat adrift on a sea of decline and loss. That's why it made sense for Urata to chant it as David Kidd's palace was coming down, and for Marguerite Yourcenar to hold it as she lay dying in her hospital bed in France.

A Thumbnail History of Buddhist Thought

The Heart Sutra is a primer of Buddhism, providing an easy-to-remember digest of the key ideas, and this has been another reason for its enduring popularity. So before we begin, let's take a brief look at those key ideas.

In India in the sixth century BC, the historical Buddha Shakyamuni (better known in the West by his birth name Siddhartha Gautama) began with the concept that life is about suffering and impermanence. He preached that we can escape from suffering by following the 'Noble Way', a life of good practice, through which we can reach a transcendent state called nirvana.

It's as simple as that in theory, and the Heart Sutra is saying more or less what the Buddha said right at the beginning. But of course, it's not so simple. Around roughly the first century AD,

Buddhism began to split into the two big divisions that we see today: Theravada and Mahayana. Theravada, the more conservative strain, focuses on Shakyamuni's early teachings.

Mahayana, basing itself on later sutras, added the concept of the bodhisattva – someone who has achieved the enlightenment of a buddha, is ready to enter nirvana, but who turns back, making a vow to wait until all sentient beings have been saved. Theravada remains strong in South East Asia and Sri Lanka. Mahayana spread north-east into Tibet, China, Korea and Japan.

The Heart Sutra belongs to Mahayana Buddhism. It focuses on one key Mahayana idea, *sunyata* or 'emptiness', propounded most forcefully by the Indian philosopher Nagarjuna in the second/third century AD. Nagarjuna stressed that not only are the things of this world transient (as Shakyamuni had taught), they are completely empty. Nothing can be said to truly exist.

And yet clearly *something* does exist, since we live in a physical world. Nagarjuna's solution was to argue that there are 'Two Truths': physical reality as we experience it is a 'lower truth', not the ultimate truth, which is emptiness. He preached accepting existence and emptiness – the lower and higher truths – at the same time. So they named his school the 'Middle Way'.

'Middle Way' sounds moderate and manageable. But Nagarjuna's 'to be and not to be' contains within it an ineradicable paradox. Generations of Buddhists, from anchorites immured in caves in Tibet, to Zen monks meditating in Kyoto, have devoted their lives to solving it. *Sunyata* proved to be one of the richest concepts in human history. The vast forest of Perfection of Wisdom sutras, and countless courtyards of empty Zen gardens, grew from this single seed.

Debate and Logic

You could call the spirit of argument a core principle of Buddhism. In other religions, when rabbis argue over what constitutes the Sabbath, or mullahs pronounce on what's lawful under Islam, there's plenty of debate. But it's all based on sacred texts and divine revelation. It comes down to what was written in the holy book.

For the Buddhists, there never was just one book – they had only an amorphous body of sutras that kept growing as people added to it. There is no Pope, no final authority to decide everything. So they drew instead on the rules of logic. The Buddha and his followers tried to show how every concept followed logically from the previous one and led inexorably to the next. A implies B, and B results in C, D and E. But it doesn't stop there. Looking at it more closely, we see that there are five types of A, and six steps in the process of B, and on it goes.

To study Buddhism, therefore, is to study lists. The earliest lists originated in the words of the Buddha himself: the Four Noble Truths, the Five Aggregates, the Six Sensory Bases and so on. Monks honed their skills in monastic debates of the sort that Xuanzang so enjoyed when he was in India, and in the process they came up with more lists.

As the lists proliferated, so did the sutras. The records show that in China over a thousand years from the third to the thirteenth century, 173 translators rendered more than 1,700

Buddhist sutras in well over 6,000 scrolls. The sutras, the lists and the fine points of argument mounted up until finally nobody could keep track of it any longer. That's when the Heart Sutra came into its own.

Gods, Buddhas and Bodhisattvas

So far, we have been talking about Buddhism as philosophy. But it's also a religion. Shakyamuni Buddha's focus was on impermanence and its logical results. He didn't talk much about spirits or the afterlife. At the same time, his thought embraced the existence of Hindu gods and goddesses, just as Christianity cocoons within it Judaism in the Old Testament.

After the historical Buddha died, there grew up the belief that earlier buddhas had lived before him, and others would come later, notably Maitreya, Buddha of the Future. So in fact there are many buddhas, not just one. After the first century AD, a gorgeous firework display of divinities exploded into being with the advent of Mahayana Buddhism. It was sparked by the concept of the bodhisattva.

The bodhisattva path, as people had originally conceived it, was one that could be pursued by anyone; it was a thoroughly human ideal. However, it was a short step from there to the idea that bodhisattvas have attained divine superpowers in order to save us. Popular bodhisattvas include Avalokiteshvara (known as Kannon in Japan), god of compassion, who features as the speaker of the Heart Sutra. Another important bodhisattva is Manjusri, god of wisdom; and there are numerous others. Kannon has a thousand arms to save us; Manjusri carries a flaming sword to cut through ignorance.

Mantras

Older than the bodhisattvas, and even older than the Buddha, are mantras, magical words or syllables that have a four-thousand-year history in India. It was believed that each syllable of the old Sanskrit alphabet had occult power.

Mantras were there at the start and still feature in Theravada Buddhism in South East Asia, such as the Thai incantation *Namo Buddhaya* ('Homage to the Buddha'). In that case the intent is clear, but often mantras consist of just a string of sounds without meaning. The eighteenth-century Zen monk Hakuin used to exclaim *'Onsoro!'* when he was making an important point, though nobody knows what this mantra actually means.

Mantras became a big feature of Buddhism in China, Tibet and Japan, and in time the syllables came to be seen as divine in and of themselves, 'seeds' from which buddhas spring into being as we speak them. The last lines of the Heart Sutra consist of a mantra, described as the supreme mantra of all. In fact the whole sutra was seen as a sort of mantra. It's believed that even if you don't understand a word of the sutra, reciting it or copying it out as calligraphy brings power.

The Heart of It All

The intense brevity of the Heart Sutra appealed even to those who had denied sutras, the followers of Zen. At the centre of it is the ideal of wisdom that is proclaimed in the full title, 'Heart of Perfected Wisdom Sutra'. The Heart Sutra condenses all the teachings about wisdom into a string of epigrams, a necklace of jewels, each one containing a world of thought. You could expand any one of them into a sutra of 100,000 lines.

Kukai, eighth/ninth-century founder of Japanese Shingon Buddhism, wrote in his commentary on the Heart Sutra: 'A discussion of each sound and letter would take eons of time and still not be complete, and buddhas equal in numbers to the motes of dust in the universe or drops of water in the oceans would still not be able to finish explaining each word and the reality it teaches.'

So condensed is the sutra that generations of thinkers have felt drawn to unpack it all over again. Like diamond merchants in Antwerp examining the lustre of a gem against the background of a scrap of pale blue paper, they pick up each jewel-phrase one by one, peer at it through a magnifying glass, and try to explain to themselves and others what it really means.

Making the job harder is the fact that there are two versions of the Heart Sutra: the 'long' one used in India, Nepal and Tibet; and the 'short' one used everywhere else. (Note that 'long' and 'short' in the case of the Heart Sutra mean only a difference of about twenty lines. They should not be confused with the 'long', 'medium' and 'short' versions of the Perfection of Wisdom sutras, each of which has thousands of lines.) The 'long' Heart Sutra is mostly the same as the 'short' Heart Sutra, with the addition of a few lines at the beginning and the end. These give context to the story, describing the scene when the Buddha, seated on Vulture Peak before his myriads of disciples, was asked by one of them, Shariputra, how to follow the path of wisdom.

In Tibet, those extra paragraphs have led to fruitful ideas not found elsewhere. While I mostly rely on the 'short' version used in Japan, sometimes I turn to the Tibetan 'long' version for insight.

Ten Parts

Short as it is, the Heart Sutra can nonetheless be divided into chapters. Commentators have split the Heart Sutra into a story with five, or seven, or ten parts. Kukai did it in five. His first chapter was the 'Opening', and each of the following parts represented one rung higher on the ladder of enlightenment. The last chapter, of course, was the mantra. My version consists of ten parts, the number of subdivisions popular in India and Tibet. For each of the ten parts, I've added a preface describing the general drift of that section.

Within each part, I take up the story line by line, as is traditional. Actually, a 'line' is an artificial concept in the case of the Heart Sutra, which consists of strings or 'phrases' of Chinese/Japanese characters, each bearing meaning in their own right. You can cut the 'phrases' in various ways, so the number of 'lines' can be as low as fifty and as high as sixty. In my version of the sutra, it comes to fifty-six lines. When commenting on the text, I often disregard lines and phrases, to highlight a fragment or even just one character. This too is traditional. Commentators from the Tang dynasty to the present have felt free to vary their focus. They might sometimes speak of the broad significance of a 'part', and other times home in on the meaning of a 'line' or focus on a single word.

A Memoir

When I first made a start on the Heart Sutra, I planned on doing a basic translation of the text and adding a selection of what commentators had said about it over time. However, as I wrote, memories and conversations with friends bubbled up within me, and I realized that our own lives were so entangled with the Heart Sutra that I couldn't separate the two.

Looking at the literature, I found that I'm not the only one to feel an intimate personal bond with the sutra. Japanese authors have published books with titles along the lines of *My Own Heart Sutra* or even *A Heart Sutra Only for Me*. Kazuaki Tanahashi's book on the subject, *The Heart Sutra: A Comprehensive Guide to the Classic of Mahayana Buddhism*, while encyclopedic in its coverage of history and philology, is filled with personal memories. It opens with a scene from 1964, when Tanahashi, before he became internationally known as a calligrapher and writer, first travelled outside Japan. In Hawaii he joined a meditation group and, finding them reciting the Heart Sutra, wondered, 'What could this mean?' From there on, Tanahashi's experience of the Heart Sutra was bound up with his own life journey.

On my part, I ended up weaving a piece of cloth in which the ideas of commentators over the centuries are the warp, the threads that run from top to bottom. My friends and our memories are the weft woven across it. I picked up a piece of string from here, a ribbon from there, and slipped them into the weave as I went along.

Pronunciation

The characters of the text (which are called *kanji* in Japanese) all originally came from China. Japan adopted the Chinese writing system, and in the Japanese version of the Heart Sutra the Chinese characters are used in the same order and with exactly the same meanings that they would have in China. However, the Japanese pronounce the *kanji* in their own way. Throughout the text, I've used the Japanese pronunciation. It's the version I'm used to, having lived most of my life in Japan.

It happens that Japanese has one great advantage over Mandarin. Since the Tang dynasty monk Xuanzang was the first to translate the sutra from Sanskrit, and only later did it come to Japan, it would seem logical to use Chinese pronunciation. But Mandarin of today is far removed from Chinese as it was spoken in Xuanzang's time. Over the centuries it has been 'rubbed down' so that final consonants have largely disappeared. In Japan, on the other hand, pronunciation underwent fewer changes. The Japanese added extra vowels at the end (*sok* became *soku*, *shik* became *shiki* and so on), staying closer to the Chinese readings of Xuanzang's time, and hence closer to the original Sanskrit.

We can see the difference in the transliteration of the title 'Great Perfection of Wisdom':

Sanskrit: *Maha Prajna Paramita*
Japanese: *Maka Hannya Haramita*
Mandarin: *Mohe Bore Boluomida*

Calligraphy

Thick and thin, dry and wet – the brushstroke of a Chinese or Japanese calligrapher transmits the writer's inner soul to paper, like a seismograph needle recording an earthquake hundreds of kilometres away. Calligraphy expresses things that can't be put into words.

But of course, calligraphy is in fact words. Each character *means* something. It was against this background that calligraphy and the Heart Sutra came to be inseparably linked. In the last years of Xuanzang's life, the reigning emperor wrote a preface to the Heart Sutra, and the next emperor had the sutra together with the preface carved on a stone stele. That monument, set up in 672, established the paradigm of 'Heart Sutra = calligraphy'.

From there on, copying out the Heart Sutra has been regarded as a pious act. Emperors would order courtiers to produce hundreds or even thousands of copies, the finest being brushed in gold letters on blue paper, like Yourcenar's fan. Old temples in Nara and Kyoto still have sutra-copying rooms where people sit at little tables outfitted with ink, brushes and lined paper, writing out the sutra. It has been the ambition of every calligrapher to produce a perfect copy.

That's why Yourcenar and I thought to pair calligraphy with text, and why I've added calligraphies to this book.

The Heart Sutra

English Translation

[Part 1]

The Great *Hannya Haramita* Heart Sutra

The Bodhisattva Who Sees Freely
Was deeply practising *Hannya Haramita*, and at that time
He saw that the Five Baskets are all empty,
And he passed beyond all pain and difficulty.

[Part 2]

Oh Shariputra!
The material world does not differ from emptiness.
Emptiness does not differ from the material world.
The material world is itself emptiness.
Emptiness is itself the material world.
Sensation, Thought, Action and Consciousness
Are all just like this.

[Part 3]

Oh Shariputra!
All these ways of being are empty appearances.
Not arising, not extinguished.
Not sullied, not pure.
Not increasing, not decreasing.

Japanese Reading

[Part 1]

摩訶般若波羅蜜多心経   *Maka Hannya Haramita*
Shingyo

観自在菩薩   *Kanjizai Bosatsu*
行深般若波羅蜜多時   *Gyo jin Hannya Haramita ji*
照見五蘊皆空   *Shoken go-on kai ku*
度一切苦厄。   *Do issai kuyaku.*

[Part 2]

舍利子。   *Sharishi.*
色不異空、   *Shiki bu i ku,*
空不異色。   *Ku bu i shiki.*
色即是空、   *Shiki soku ze ku,*
空即是色。   *Ku soku ze shiki.*
受・想・行・識   *Ju so gyo shiki*
亦復如是。   *Yaku bu nyoze.*

[Part 3]

舍利子。   *Sharishi.*
是諸法空相   *Ze shoho ku so*
不生不滅、   *Fusho fumetsu,*
不垢不浄、   *Fuku fujo,*
不増不減。   *Fuzo fugen.*

[Part 4]

Therefore, within this emptiness
There is no material world.
There is no Sensation, Thought, Action or Consciousness.
No eyes, ears, nose, tongue, body or mind.
No colour, sound, scent, taste, touch or *dharmas*.

[Part 5]

There is no world of sight,
And the same for the rest; there is no world of consciousness.
There is no ignorance.
And, likewise, there is no end to ignorance.
And the same for the rest; there is no ageing and death.
Likewise, there is no end to ageing and death.

[Part 6]

There is no Suffering, nor Causes of Suffering,
Nor Cessation of Suffering, nor the Noble Way.
There is no wisdom.
Likewise, there's nothing to be gained.
And because there is nothing to be gained . . .

[Part 7]

The bodhisattvas
Rely on *Hannya Haramita* and therefore
The heart is without encumbrance.
And because it is without encumbrance,
There is nothing to fear or worry about.

[Part 4]

是故空中、	*Ze ko ku chu,*
無色、	*Mu shiki,*
無受・想・行・識。	*Mu ju so gyo shiki.*
無眼・耳・鼻・舌・身・意、	*Mu gen ni bi ze shin i,*
無色・声・香・味・触・法。	*Mu shiki sho ko mi soku ho.*

[Part 5]

無眼界、	*Mu genkai,*
乃至、無意識界。	*Naishi mu ishiki kai.*
無無明、	*Mu mumyo,*
亦無無明尽。	*Yaku mu mumyo jin.*
乃至、無老死、	*Naishi, mu roshi,*
亦無老死尽。	*Yaku mu roshi jin.*

[Part 6]

無苦・集	*Mu ku shu*
滅・道。	*Metsu do.*
無智、	*Mu chi,*
亦無得。	*Yaku mu toku.*
以無所得故 . . .	*I mu shotoku ko . . .*

[Part 7]

菩提薩埵	*Bodaisatta*
依般若波羅蜜多故、	*E Hannya Haramita ko,*
心無罣礙。	*Shin mu kege.*
無罣礙故、	*Mu kege ko,*
無有恐怖。	*Mu u kufu.*

27

[Part 8]

They escape all absurdities and fantasies,
Reaching ultimate nirvana.
The buddhas of the Three Worlds
Rely on *Hannya Haramita*, and therefore
They attain supreme, perfect enlightenment.

[Part 9]

Thus they know that *Hannya Haramita*
Is the mantra of great mystery.
It is the mantra of great light.
It is the mantra of which none is higher.
It is the mantra ranked beyond all ranks.
With it one escapes all suffering.
It is truth and reality, without falsehood.

[Part 10]

Therefore we chant the mantra of *Hannya Haramita*.
Now we chant, saying:
Gyatei gyatei,
Hara gyatei,
Hara so gyatei,
Bodai sowaka.

Heart of Wisdom Sutra

[Part 8]

遠離一切顛倒夢想、	*Onri issai tendo muso,*
究竟涅槃。	*Kugyo nehan.*
三世諸仏	*Sanze shobutsu*
依般若波羅蜜多故、	*E Hannya Haramita ko,*
得阿耨多羅、三藐三菩提。	*Toku anokutara, sanmyaku*
	sanbodai.

[Part 9]

故知、般若波羅蜜多	*Ko chi, Hannya Haramita*
是大神呪、	*Ze dai jinshu,*
是大明呪、	*Ze dai myoshu,*
是無上呪、	*Ze mujoshu,*
是無等等呪。	*Ze mutodoshu.*
能除一切苦、	*No jo issai ku,*
真実不虚。	*Shinjitsu fu ko.*

[Part 10]

故説、般若波羅蜜多呪。	*Ko setsu, Hannya Haramita shu.*
即説呪曰、	*Soku setsu shu watsu,*
羯諦羯諦、	*Gyatei, gyatei,*
波羅羯諦、	*Hara gyatei,*
波羅僧羯諦、	*Hara so gyatei,*
菩提薩婆訶。	*Bodai sowaka.*

般若心経	*Hannya Shingyo*

PART I

The Opening

摩訶般若波羅蜜多心経	The Great Hannya Haramita Heart Sutra
観自在菩薩	The Bodhisattva Who Sees Freely
行深般若波羅蜜多時	Was deeply practising Hannya Haramita, and at that time
照見五蘊皆空	He saw that the Five Baskets are all empty,
度一切苦厄。	And he passed beyond all pain and difficulty.

The sutra begins by invoking its name, 'The Great *Hannya Haramita* Heart Sutra'. This puts us in the mood for reciting something sacred and familiar, preparing us to listen again to the story we have heard so many times before.

In the longer Tibetan version, the sutra opens with the Buddha seated on the top of Vulture Peak. Below sit a host of followers awaiting his words. The Buddha's closest disciple, Shariputra, asks: 'What is the Perfection of Wisdom?'

The Buddha, deep in meditation, turns to Kannon, bodhi-sattva of compassion, and asks him to answer in his stead. Kannon, who almost never speaks in any other sutra, does so. He's channelling the Buddha's meditation, which is so removed, so far beyond anything, that the Buddha himself cannot express it.

Kannon tells Shariputra that he has practised the Perfection of Wisdom, and he has found that all the things of this world are empty. Kannon gets to the point – emptiness – within the first few lines. It's the knot of wisdom that the rest of the sutra is devoted to unravelling.

摩訶

Maka – The Great

Given how short it is, it's curious that this sutra is called 'great'. The word in the original Sanskrit is *maha*, the root of English words such as 'magnitude' and 'magnificent'.

The early Chinese compilers chose to use *maha* and not the usual Chinese character 大 (*da*) for 'great'. It was part of their rule of 'things not to be translated', which they applied to Sanskrit words that had no counterpart in China. The Chinese *da* meant merely 'big', a day-to-day word without much romance about it. *Maha*, in contrast, sounds rather exotic and suggests something immeasurably big. Vast.

Commentators have made much about this word 'vast'. Indeed the Heart Sutra, when you first come across it, is like a sudden discovery of uncharted continents and hidden oceans one hadn't known existed. But why do we have to dwell on it being so vast? 'Great', as in, for example, 'Great Britain', can refer to things that are rather small. In the eighteenth century, Hakuin wrote a colourful commentary called *Poison Words on the Heart Sutra*. In it he remarks: 'Most folks think *maha* means large and vast – and they are all wrong! Bring me a *small* wisdom! '

As Hakuin realized, most of us are not going to become monks and give up everything to learn the cumulated wisdom of the ages. We just need something small, a useful idea or two to help us in our daily lives. The Heart Sutra is so short you can recite the whole thing in about a minute. It's a haiku of wisdom, wisdom you can carry in your back pocket.

般若

Hannya – Wisdom

Hannya is the Chinese reading of *prajna*, a Sanskrit term meaning 'wisdom'. Xuanzang, rather than trying to put it into understandable Chinese, left it as it was, the transliterated sound of *prajna*, rather than its meaning. He said *hannya* is so profound as to be untranslatable.

Since *hannya* is the core concept of the Heart Sutra, there's a temptation among writers to try to explain it right at the outset. However, I follow Xuanzang in not attempting to make sense of it. Instead, this is the moment to visualize Manjusri, bodhisattva of wisdom.

Everyone has a personal guardian deity. For Xuanzang, translator of the Heart Sutra, it was Kannon, bodhisattva of compassion. For me, it has been Manjusri, ever since David Kidd first introduced him to me in 1973.

In the old days when David still had his palace, everything happened at night. Around dusk, friends would start to gather, and during the evening David would display treasures in the wide living room. Seated on his broad *kang* throne, he would drink endless cups of tea while chatting with guests as we probed the secrets of artworks.

It was the early 1970s, and we were all into heightened consciousness and psychedelic colours. David, who had discovered Tibet and its mystical art, owned a large Tibetan painting of the *Kalachakra*, the Wheel of Time. He was always into gadgetry, and after we had gazed on the great painting for a while, he had a replica – painted on a vinyl sheet and mounted on a mechanized stand – brought into the room. The room was plunged into darkness, and then we could see phosphorescent colors glowing under black light, as the motorized Wheel of Time turned, accompanied by a version of Pachelbel's Canon performed on a synthesizer.

Shimmering in the black light stood one of David's Tibetan statues, of the bodhisattva Manjusri, a boyish figure seated on a lotus, holding books in one hand and a flaming sword in the other. David revered Manjusri as the patron of wisdom and the arts. The books symbolize knowledge, and the flaming sword is to cut through ignorance.

Later, when I became acquainted with the Heart Sutra, I discovered that although he is not mentioned by name, Manjusri is there, floating invisibly above the words. For Kukai, Manjusri is the 'thinker' behind the entire *Hannya Haramita* corpus – long, medium and short. In Kukai's words: 'The sutras of the Great *Hannya Haramita* – in one compilation, six hundred scrolls, sixteen chapters, and two hundred and eighty-two folios – these are all the gate to the meditation of Manjusri.'

At Tibetan or Bhutanese temples you will see an image of a flaming sword. It's Manjusri's blade slashing through ignorance.

波羅蜜多

Haramita – Perfection

As they did with *maha* and *hannya*, the early Chinese translators of the Heart Sutra left *paramita* (*haramita* in the Japanese
reading) in the original Sanskrit. The word started out as a
combination of *para* ('the other shore') and *mita* ('to arrive') –
that is, 'arrived at the other shore'. From this, the word *paramita*
came to mean 'perfection'.

Derived from a literal sense of 'arrival', *Hannya Haramita*
('Perfection of Wisdom') implies not just a state of having
understood something, but a journey. Since the eighth century,
commentators have likened it to a boat, carrying us from 'this
shore' (the world of illusion and sorrow) to the 'other shore'
(enlightenment and nirvana).

Hannya Haramita is both the destination, the 'other shore',
and the boat you are sailing in. Upon uttering the words
Hannya Haramita, you have sounded a nautical whistle as they
used to do in the old days when the captain boarded a ship.
You've walked up the gangplank, and they've stowed it away.
They've cast off the lines and the boat has pulled away from
the dock. Now you're headed out to sea.

心

Shin – Heart

Zen monk Hasunuma Ryochoku of Nanzenji Temple in Kyoto contends that the standard English translation of *shin* 心 as 'heart' is wrong, and we should not be calling this the 'Heart Sutra'. The sutra contains the compressed essence of all the teachings on wisdom, so 'heart' in this case should be read as 'summation' or 'essence'. The correct title would be 'The Essence Sutra'.

That said, they *did* use the word 'heart', when there might have been other ways to say 'essence'. We can probably blame Xuanzang, the first translator. He chose this word and, as a result, readers and commentators for the last twelve hundred years have ended up thinking about the heart.

In Chinese and Japanese, *shin* means both 'heart' and 'mind', referring both to what we think and what we feel. It might not be a coincidence that the school of Buddhism that personally attracted Xuanzang and later went on to influence Zen was called 'Mind Only' 唯識. It teaches that the only thing that truly exists is one's own heart or mind.

If there is one book in the Western tradition that is closest in spirit to the Heart Sutra it's a short manual compiled from the work of the Greek philosopher Epictetus. His sayings were handed down by his disciple Arrian during the second century AD in a little volume entitled *Enchiridion*, meaning 'a handbook'. In later times, this brief guide to Stoic wisdom went on to have a huge impact on the Western Enlightenment, being found in the libraries of such prominent figures as Rabelais, Adam Smith and Thomas Jefferson.

The first line of the *Enchiridion* reads: 'There are things which are within our power, and there are things which are beyond our power.' Things beyond our power, according to Epictetus, are all the external objects around us and the events of the world. They come and go and we have no power over them; the only thing over which we have any control is our own minds.

The Heart Sutra, too, teaches that in the end there's nothing outside ourselves that we may cling on to. This realization, which might seem rather bleak, can also be a source of strength. The principle of reliance on one's own heart or mind is what led Yourcenar to keep that fan with her until her dying day.

経

Gyo – Sutra

The word for sutra (*jing* in Chinese, *kyo* or *gyo* in Japanese) originally meant 'thread', in reference to the threads used for tying together the pages of a book. The Chinese used this at first to name the Confucian classics, such as the *Yi-jing* or 'Book of Changes' (usually known in English as the *I Ching*), *Shi-jing* or 'Classic of Poetry', and so forth. Along came Buddhism, imported from India after the first century AD, and the Chinese translators borrowed this word to mean a Buddhist scripture.

In the early days of Buddhism's transmission to China, there was a deep thirst for sutras, which were thought to be the most precious things in the world. That's what propelled Xuanzang on his sixteen-year quest to India. In AD 645, Xuanzang returned to Chang'an with his vast collection of sutras, hundreds of texts in dozens of boxes loaded onto the backs of horses in a great cavalcade. Tens of thousands of people lined the roads of the capital to witness the triumphal arrival of the sutras from the West. And among them all, written down on one small scrap of paper, was the Heart Sutra. It was Xuanzang's personal prayer.

The sixteenth-century Chinese novel *Journey to the West* describes how Xuanzang and his magical companions Monkey and Pig, after many arduous years spent crossing deserts and mountains, finally arrive at the heavenly abode of the Buddha. When they ask for sutras to take back east to the Tang court,

Buddha instructs his disciples Ananda and Kasyapa, keepers of the library, to hand them over. However, back at the library, Ananda and Kasyapa demand a bribe, and when Xuanzang refuses to pay it, they give him rolls of blank paper – wordless sutras – instead.

Having discovered the ruse, Xuanzang returns with Pig and Monkey to the Buddha's palace where Monkey angrily denounces the keepers of the library for giving them empty sutras. 'Stop yelling,' replies the Lord Buddha with a smile. 'You were given blank texts because you came here to fetch them empty-handed. The blank texts are true, wordless scriptures, and they really are good. But as you living beings in the East are so deluded and have not achieved enlightenment we'll have to give you these ones instead.'

Ananda and Kasyapa hand over a new set of sutras, but only after Xuanzang agrees to give them his golden begging bowl in exchange. That, according to *Journey to the West*, is how Xuanzang finally got the sutras he then brought back to the Tang emperor in China.

Sutras don't come for free. And the sutras that Xuanzang brought back, for all their profundity, are not the ultimate ones. They're just replacements for the originals still in the Buddha's library, which have no words.

観自在菩薩

Kanjizai Bosatsu – The Bodhisattva Who Sees Freely

The 'Bodhisattva Who Sees Freely' is Avalokiteshvara, bodhisattva of compassion.

There's a quirk here about the translation. In most other sutras – and in almost every Chinese or Japanese temple today – Avalokiteshvara is called Kannon 観音 (Guanyin in Chinese), which means 'Perceiving the Sounds (of the World)'. 'Perceiving the Sounds' was the rendering that the early Chinese translators came up with, and it has remained popular because it's such an evocative way of conveying compassion. But Xuanzang, who was a rather dry scholarly type, went back to the original Sanskrit wording of Avalokiteshvara's name for his translation.

Avalokita (from *ava*, which means 'away' or 'down', and *lokita*, which is related to the English word 'look') means 'to see' (*kan* 観 in Chinese). The second part of the name, *ishvara* (or *eshvara*), means 'lord' or 'mighty'. From this derives the sense of 'mastery' and, by extension, 'freedom', which is how it was rendered in Chinese (*jizai* 自在). Putting these two together, Xuangzang translated the name as Kanjizai 観自在, which means 'He Who Sees Freely'. This is not so poetic as 'Perceiving the Sounds of the World', but in the case of the Heart Sutra, Xuanzang's version stuck.

We can see that Xuanzang took special pride in this translation, for when his disciple Kuiji came to write the first commentary on the Heart Sutra, he made rather a point of it. 'To call him *Guanyin* ("Perceiving Sounds") would be to misinterpret the term and to lose the meaning of his name,' he wrote. So it's worth thinking about what Xuanzang might have had in mind.

First of all, there's the sense of liberation in 'seeing freely'. Back in my college days, I bought an old thatched house in the mountains of Iya Valley on Japan's southern island of Shikoku. It had a smoky hearth in the middle of the floor, and over it hung a blackened teapot, suspended from the rafters by a long section of bamboo. The word for that bamboo was *jizai* ('free-hanging').

Years later I came across the word *jizai* again when I first tried reading the Heart Sutra by myself. Not realizing that this referred to Kannon (I thought the strange name Kanjizai must be some other bodhisattva), I interpreted it as 'The Bodhisattva Who Sees While Freely Hanging'. I imagined a bodhisattva high in the sky, swinging on a thread from a cloud. I still get a feeling of blue-skied freshness and freedom when I read these words, and I wonder if that sense of freedom was what Xuanzang was trying to express.

In addition to 'freely', *ishvara* (or *jizai*) has the sense of 'mighty', and it was the epithet given to great divinities. In particular, in later times it referred to avatars of the Hindu god Shiva. While Xuanzang himself may not have intended it, Buddhist believers came to believe that, at a mystical level, Kannon and Shiva were one. Of the Hindu gods, Shiva is the destroyer, but also the performer of the cosmic dance, shown in sculptures with one leg raised and arms and hands outstretched as he dances, the world spinning around him.

David Kidd had lived in Beijing during the last years leading up to the Communist takeover in 1949, and in the early days of his life in Japan, before he became an art dealer, he wrote a series of articles about his life in China which were picked up by the *New Yorker*. All was going well, until he attempted a non-China story. He once read it to me from a yellowing manuscript that he kept in his desk.

The story is about a middle-aged man living in the suburbs of America somewhere, who wakes up in the middle of the night. He starts to walk downstairs, but as he lowers his foot onto the next step, he suddenly transforms into the Divine Shiva. His skin turns blue, his legs and arms whirl in ecstatic dance, while a myriad shining galaxies sweep round him to an infinite distance and through infinite time. A second later, his foot touches the landing, and the vision is over. He turns at the landing, goes back upstairs and whispers goodnight to his sleeping wife. He walks downstairs and through the front door, leaving everything behind. The *New Yorker* turned it down; David Kidd never wrote another story.

As the sutra opens, the bodhisattva of compassion is about to reveal to us the emptiness of all things. But the bodhisattva of compassion is himself just an emanation of Shiva. Behind him, you can see the shadow of delirious Shiva dancing among spinning stars.

行深

Gyo jin – Was deeply practising

Gyo 行 ('practice' and also 'to practise') is what monks undergo in their training inside the temple; it's an ordeal, a trial to be mastered. And it never ends. You practise; you reach a new level; and then you practise again.

Having waited thirty years to write about the Heart Sutra, I find that in the meantime I'm now growing old. And at an age when I should know better, I find myself disappointingly still unprepared to meet new life crises as they appear. Each time a fresh problem arises, I need to revisit lessons of patience and compassion I should have learned long ago. I had thought that age would give some wisdom and relief, but no, it's never-ending *gyo*.

This word *gyo*, coming right near the beginning of the sutra, speaks of the effort involved in acquiring (and retaining) wisdom. *Gyo* passes below the radar of most commentators, who are more interested in the philosophical high notes than the grind of sheer hard work. But it might be one of the most important words in the sutra.

Kuiji, Xuanzang's student who wrote the first commentary on the Heart Sutra, devoted many pages, over a third of his text, to this one idea. For Kuiji, the Heart Sutra is, above all things, an 'encouragement to practise'.

As an added dimension, *gyo* does not just mean 'to practise'; its basic sense is 'to walk', 'to go' and, by extension, 'to
reach', 'to penetrate'. Another way to read this line is: 'Had
penetrated to the deepest *Hannya Haramita*'. 'Practise' implies
the hard work of it. 'Penetrate' suggests travelling to the fur-
thest reaches, until you finally grasp the pearl hidden in a shell
on the ocean floor.

In either case, the operative word here is *jin* 深 ('deep').
Kannon, the bodhisattva of compassion, has descended to the
uncharted sub-oceanic waters of wisdom, and he is about to
tell us what he has seen down there. With this word 'deep', the
sutra starts its dive into the darkness.

般若波羅蜜多

Hannya Haramita – Perfection of Wisdom

Hannya Haramita, as we've seen, means 'Perfection of Wisdom', but at this early point in the sutra these words are just obscure Sanskrit syllables. We still have no idea what Kannon is talking about.

When the sutra opens, the Buddha is deep in meditation, sunk as if in a diving bell to depths where no light can penetrate. He has found a world of utter stillness, of forms beyond forms, but it's impossible to impart this to others who know only the bright sunlight and churning waves at the surface.

Buddha has asked Kannon to try to reveal this dark world to us, and Kannon's challenge is to find words that will make sense to us. But first, before we try to probe the meaning of *Hannya Haramita*, we should meet her.

Hannya Haramita's female identity becomes clear if we look closely at the fine points of Sanskrit grammar, something that scholars of the Heart Sutra love to do. It turns out that in Sanskrit the *ta* of *paramita* is a feminine ending. That makes *Hannya Haramita* a woman. She started as a philosophical concept, but over time grew into a goddess in her own right. From Java to Angkor Wat, and all the way to Tibet, they carved statues and painted images of the goddess Hannya Haramita and worshipped her.

The Eastern Orthodox Church also worshipped the wisdom of God in female form, as Sophia. In the nineteenth and twentieth centuries, some Russian schools of mysticism even exalted Sophia to the level of the Trinity, with whom she was seen as equal, although that soon got them into trouble with the Church. Sophia went on to feature in Western spiritualism as the primal mind or mysterious intelligence which animates the universe. There seems to be an archetype within the human spirit that sees wisdom as female.

Hannya Haramita is called the 'Mother of All the Buddhas'. The early Chinese translators were so aware of this that they entitled the sutra 'The Sacred Mother Sutra', and the Tibetan title still reads: 'The Blessed Mother, Heart of the Perfection of Wisdom'.

The Indians and Tibetans have rituals by which to conjure the goddess before reciting the Heart Sutra. The eleventh-century Indian sage Darikapa wrote a verse describing the visualization of Hannya Haramita. First, you imagine in your mind's eye the peak of soaring Mount Sumeru, the centre of the universe, girdled by four continents and ringed with seven mountain ranges. The goddess is seated at the peak:

Rising from Mount Sumeru
A beautiful palace
Expansive and ornamented.
In the center of it is a lion throne
Where, seated on the lotus and the sun,
Is the orange Mother of the Conquerors, her body golden.

時

Ji – At that time

Ji is the only time word in the sutra. It's a grammatical particle meaning 'when' or 'at that time'. As a stand-alone character, it simply means 'time'. The seventh/eighth-century commentator Fazang has another interpretation of this word. He says it means not just any ordinary time, when one might speak of ordinary things, but a unique moment in a bodhisattva's spiritual progress. It means 'time' as in 'the time has come'.

In an earlier version attributed to the fifth-century Central Asian monk Kumarajiva, there is a fuller reference to time, with an extra line that reads: 'Thus, the emptiness of all ways of being has no past, no present, and no future.' While Xuanzang mostly followed Kumarajiva's wording in his translation, he cut this line in order to make the sutra truly 'timeless'. Or, as it has been suggested, he cut the line for better rhythm. Every other line of the sutra consists of balanced pairs of concepts, but 'past, present and future' involved a group of three. So they ended up on the cutting-room floor.

This reminds us of the Heart Sutra's inherent musicality. It's not only a work of philosophy, but a poem.

照見

Shoken – He saw that

Shoken 照見, translated as 'he saw' in the Heart Sutra, is an unusual combination of two words: *sho* 照 ('to shine light on') and *ken* 見 ('to see'). With this word, light enters the sutra.

After attaining enlightenment, the Buddha meditated in a cave, and the light from his body illuminated the darkness. This radiance explains why Buddhist statues are gold and sit in niches (representing the cave), and why their heads and bodies are framed with halos and swirling flames. In the Lotus Sutra, it is written that the Buddha lights up eighteen thousand worlds from a single white hair between his eyebrows.

One friend in David Kidd's circle who occupied a special place of respect, was William Gilkey, a pianist from Chikasha, Oklahoma, who lived in Beijing in the 1940s and then moved to Japan where he lived for decades in Osaka. Now dwelling in a small house in Kameoka, the town where I lived near Kyoto, Gilkey had become a sort of ancient guru to the rest of us. With his bald head, wispy beard and twinkling eyes, he looked a lot like Yoda in *Star Wars*. He had much to say about spiritual light.

Having read a massive amount of spiritualist literature, Gilkey shared its essence with me, sparing me the chore of having to read it myself. He was a psychic and a mage, which is why David treated him with such respect.

Gilkey could stop rain, and had mastered the use of other mystical techniques. But more importantly, he talked about the ways in which we can kindle our inner light. The light is so powerful that we can do a lot of good, and also harm with it. As Gilkey warned us: 'This has nothing to do with ordinary light. It's the Odic light that was never seen on land nor sea.'

We were of course more fascinated to see Gilkey stop the rain. But he would hardly ever do it, except on laundry day.

五蘊

Go-on – The Five Baskets

The first thing that the bodhisattva Kannon shines his light on are the 'Five Baskets' 五蘊. 'Baskets' was how Xuanzang translated the Sanskrit word *skandhas* (literally 'aggregates'). The Five Baskets are a Buddhist list, a key one dating back to Buddha's first sermons. The first of the five is the material world. The other four are the ways we perceive and process the material world: Sensation, Thought, Action and Consciousness.

The Buddha called these things 'aggregates' because they arise from a mixture of outside influences, change constantly and so have no reality in and of themselves. Xuanzang used the tactile word 'baskets' to put across the idea that the 'aggregates' are a 'mixed bag' of all sorts of things. They contain our lives and personalities, and also everything else that we perceive in the world around us.

Nowadays we might translate Xuanzang's 'baskets' as 'shoulder bags' or 'backpacks'. Look inside them and you will find tears and laughter, children, houses, the weather, mountains, the Earth, the universe.

皆空

Kai ku – Are all empty

Ku 空 ('emptiness') lies at the heart of the Heart Sutra.

Ku is the primal emptiness of the universe, known as *sunyata* in Sanskrit, a concept propounded by the great Buddhist philosopher Nagarjuna in the second/third century A D. Nagarjuna taught that since all things are in flux and depend on multiple unknowable causes, they are only ephemera with no real existence of their own. We are deluding ourselves if we believe that the world we live in has any inherent reality.

Nagarjuna's concept of emptiness is truly radical. But one could add that he didn't create emptiness out of nothing. The seed of emptiness lay right at the start of Buddhism, in the blissful empty state of nirvana. Nowhere does the Buddha mention a creator god. More seriously, the early Buddhists denied the existence of an eternal soul. They applied the law of impermanence to the soul, and called this *anatta*, or 'non-self'.

At this level, Buddhism reveals its profoundly atheistic roots. It was existentialism long before cigarette-smoking French philosophers in Parisian cafés started thinking about what the consequences would really be if there was no God. Buddhism, as you see it in temples, is rich with the outward symbols of worship and ritual, golden sculpture, implements in bronze and lacquer, chimes and incense. But probe Buddhist philosophy, and you will find no salvation in those things. Like everything else, they are essentially empty.

Around the time that his palace was coming down, David Kidd became involved with a Shinto-derived religion called Oomoto, based in the town of Kameoka near Kyoto, for which Gilkey and I both ended up working. Oomoto was engaged in organizing inter-religious conferences, and once sponsored a big gathering of religious leaders from around the world, at which I was one of the translators. Attendees included Buddhist monks from Thailand and Tibet, Catholic cardinals and Eastern Orthodox bishops, Muslim imams, Indian gurus and Jewish rabbis, indigenous African chiefs, and many more.

At the end of the conference, the delegates decided that they would issue a communiqué, a simple mission statement about something that everyone could agree on. It could not include the word 'God', of course, which everyone calls by a different name. A decision was made to go with the following: 'We all believe in a higher power.' Everybody was ready to sign off on that, but then the Sri Lankan Buddhists objected. 'In the end, there is no ultimate God, or higher power,' they said. 'We Buddhists believe in nothing beyond the nothingness of nirvana.'

So they had to tear up the communiqué and go home without one.

度

Do – And he passed beyond

The idea of crossing a river or the sea to the other shore reverberates throughout the sutra like an echoing gong. The first time we hear it is in *haramita* ('perfection'), derived, as we saw above, from words that mean 'arrived at the other shore'. Here, in another phrasing of the same idea, it says 'passed beyond'.

If we turn to the end of the Heart Sutra, we find there a mystical chant, *gyatei, gyatei*, which can be translated as 'crossing over to the other side'. Bracketed at the beginning with 'arrived at the other shore', and concluding with 'crossing over to the other side', the sutra is describing a journey. However, it's not an overland journey, via towns and cities, with places of interest to visit along the way. As the references to the 'other shore' indicate, it's a voyage across an open, featureless ocean to an unknown coast.

Fazang called the Heart Sutra a 'fast-moving boat over stormy seas'.

一切苦厄

Issai kuyaku – All pain and difficulty

Suffering is the first truth taught by the Buddha. The story is that when Prince Siddhartha slipped away from his protected life in the palace, he saw outside the walls an old man, a sick man and a corpse, and these inspired him to follow a life of meditation. But it didn't happen right away. First he returned to the palace for another night carousing with the women of the harem.

On the farewell day at David Kidd's palace, when we each took a swing with a mallet to bring down the plaster walls, the last thing left hanging in the reception room was a huge scroll painted in the 1920s, three metres tall and two metres wide. Seated on a throne in the middle of the painting is a handsome young man, Prince Siddhartha, with a thoughtful look on his face. At his feet are the women, who had all suddenly fallen asleep, according to legend. They are voluptuous, bare-breasted, with pink flesh and painted nails. Above him, clad in brown monkish robes, float ghostly bodhisattvas, beckoning him away to a purer life.

In the painting, the virile young Buddha-to-be is perfectly balanced between the pleasures of the flesh that he has just enjoyed, and the renunciation that he has just decided upon. It's a sensual image that shows utter climax and satiation, and, in the same moment, the resolve to leave it all. That quizzical expression in the young Buddha's eyes is the realization that the pleasure he has just experienced is transitory, and the reality he must face from now on is the suffering he witnessed outside the palace walls.

Ageing, sickness and death. Given the Buddha's teaching that we have no eternal soul, given that there is no glorious heaven or all-knowing God to receive us, but only the emptiness of nirvana, how are we to deal with suffering?

The answer lies in emptiness itself.

PART 2

The Material World and Emptiness are the Same

舎利子。	Oh Shariputra!
色不異空、	The material world does not differ from emptiness.
空不異色。	Emptiness does not differ from the material world.
色即是空、	The material world is itself emptiness.
空即是色。	Emptiness is itself the material world.
受・想・行・識	Sensation, Thought, Action and Consciousness
亦復如是。	Are all just like this.

Not everyone can recite the whole Heart Sutra from memory, but if they know anything about it at all, they will usually be aware of these four lines, the ones that the kabuki audience instantly recognized:

The material world does not differ from emptiness.
Emptiness does not differ from the material world.
The material world is itself emptiness.
Emptiness is itself the material world.

'The material world' (known as *rupa* in Sanskrit) is the first of the Five Baskets. It stands in contrast to *sunyata*, the great emptiness that lies behind everything. *Rupa* is our world of the senses, love, sex, happiness, sickness and sorrow – and looking beyond us, everything in the physical world, day and night, galaxies and space-time itself appearing and disappearing – all awash in a heaving sea of impermanence. This is the frenzied cosmic dance of Shiva. It's one great kaleidoscopic illusion, but it's where we live our lives.

Sunyata, in contrast to *rupa*, is the realm of pure spirituality, hovering beyond everything material. It's quiet, pure, empty. It's the nothingness that seems to be at the core of subatomic particles; it's the big blank that's left at the moment of death.

These four lines sum up Nagarjuna's concept of Two Truths, namely: *'rupa' and 'sunyata' are the same thing.*

That's easy enough to say, but suppose, for example, that you are trying to help your sick child, or fighting for a just cause that will make the world better – should you just walk away because you know that it's all empty in the end?

On the other hand, if the materialism of the world is all there is, then perhaps we should just give in and worship money, sex and power, and accept that this is it. But we know in our souls that this is not right.

The Tibetans call these four lines the 'Four Profundities'. Actually it's just one profundity, repeated in four different ways so it can sink in. It is the intractable enigma at the heart of this text, the idea that launched a thousand sutras.

The sutra goes on to add: 'Sensation, Thought, Action and Consciousness are all just like this.' Not only is the material world outside us empty and an illusion, but everything we think and feel is too.

舍利子

Sharishi – Oh Shariputra!

Shariputra was one of Buddha's closest and best-loved disciples. He's the one who asked the question about 'Perfection of Wisdom', so the answer is addressed to him.

Twice Kannon calls out to Shariputra, reminding us that the Heart Sutra is not an essay written down on paper, but words spoken from one person to another. It's a conversation, not a lecture. And as with any conversation, the transmission is imperfect.

Shariputra was not a good debater. He's depicted in Buddhist writings sometimes as the wisest of all the disciples, and at other times as a dullard of limited wits, his arguments crushed by people who are cleverer than him. In one sutra, Shariputra debates with a celestial maiden on the subject of whether a woman could ever be enlightened. Shariputra thinks it's going to be an easy win, but the celestial maiden turns the tables on him by transforming Shariputra himself into a celestial maiden. She challenges him to change from a woman back into a man, but he can't do it.

Poor Shariputra, easily tricked and deluded, stands for us, the imperfect readers and reciters of the sutra today.

色

Shiki – The material world

When Westernization came to Japan after the country opened up to the world in the 1860s, it posed a huge challenge in translation. Thousands of Western words, such as 'freedom', 'politics', 'economics', 'diplomacy', 'electricity', 'train' and so on, simply had no counterpart, so the early translators had to come up with creative ways of expressing them. China modernized a few decades later, so many modern Chinese words may actually be traced back to nineteenth-century Japan.

The transmission of Buddhist thought to China required an even bigger translation effort that involved hundreds of translators working over half a millennium. The early Chinese translators grappled with how to translate arcane Indian philosophical concepts like *anatta* ('non-self') and nirvana. One of the most difficult to put into Chinese was *rupa* ('the material world').

Rupa implies tangible objects like fire and water; feelings such as love and anger; cravings for beauty, wealth or power. In a stroke of poetic brilliance, the translators decided on the character 色, pronounced *shiki* in Japanese. *Shiki* literally means 'colour'. It can also mean 'sex'. That's why in the kabuki play *Dojoji*, when the dancing girl dressed in a flamboyant red kimono uses this expression, she does it with a seductive smile. 'Colour' and 'sex' are viscerally physical, so it's the perfect word to stand for *rupa*, 'the material world'. As a good

Buddhist, you are not supposed to be swayed by pretty people, money or bright colours, but of course we all are. So the word 'colour' has quite a bit of mischief attached to it.

The phrase that begins with *Shiki* reads: 'The material world does not differ from emptiness.' This and the following three lines are the burning core of the Heart Sutra. Nagarjuna taught that while ultimately all is emptiness, we should not give into nihilism. That would be too easy. Emptiness is but one side of the story. The material world is the other side, and we need to hold them both in our minds at the same time.

Tibetan monk Geshe Sonam Rinchen says that it is as if we were walking along a narrow path with an abyss on one side and a cliff covered in barbed wire on the other. If we choose nihilism, we plunge into the abyss. If we cling too closely to the cliff, we get caught on the barbed wire of our messy lives. After that, we can neither move forward nor go back the way we came. We are stuck.

不異空

Bu i ku – Does not differ from emptiness

'Emptiness' does not mean that the universe is empty. This question has long vexed philosophers in the West as well as the East. In eighteenth-century London, when the topic of non-existence came up in a conversation between Samuel Johnson and James Boswell, Johnson kicked a stone so hard he rebounded from it, to show that physical things are very real. But Nagarjuna would see that stone as 'empty' nonetheless, because things – even the hardest stones – lack enduring substance.

The term for this that you often come across in Buddhist writings is 'dependent origination' 因縁. That's a way of saying that everything depends on something else. Stones come into existence in the flow of lava and the piling up of sediment; and they wear away with water and wind. They are made of chemicals with emergent properties derived from atomic bonds and electromagnetic fields, and they are bound by gravity which depends on the earth and the pull of its orbit around the sun. The stone's weight, colour and positioning at the right spot to be kicked came about because of causes external to it. A lot of things had to happen to bring that stone in contact with Dr Johnson's foot at just the right moment. The deeper you look into it, the more ungraspable and nebulous a stone becomes.

Instead of using the cumbrous phrase 'dependent origination', Vietnamese monk Thich Nhat Hanh calls this 'inter-being'. Holding up a sheet of paper, he says:

> If you are a poet, you will see clearly that there is a cloud floating in this sheet of paper. Without a cloud, there can be no rain; without rain, the trees cannot grow; and without trees, we cannot make paper. The cloud is essential for the paper to exist. If the cloud is not here, the sheet of paper cannot be here either. So we can say that the cloud and the paper *inter-are*.

In the old days – that is, right up until the 1970s – it was assumed that causality was pretty straightforward. Clouds lead to rain, which leads to trees, which lead to paper. Fittingly, it happened to be the study of clouds that led to some startling conclusions. Meteorologist Edward Lorenz showed that clouds are 'sensitive to initial conditions' – that is, only a tiny change at one point can have massive impact further afield. He called it the 'butterfly effect', according to which the flap of a butterfly's wings in Brazil could set off a tornado in Texas.

Once the mathematicians and physicists got to work on it, they realized that 'sensitivity to initial conditions' is at work everywhere, not only in the weather, but in practically every event in the universe. It seems absurd. Surely big things produce big effects, and small things small effects? But it turns out it doesn't work that way. We can see 'sensitivity to initial conditions' in action in an old English rhyme:

> For want of a nail the shoe was lost.
> For want of a shoe the horse was lost.
> For want of a horse the rider was lost.

For want of a rider the message was lost.
For want of a message the battle was lost.
For want of a battle the kingdom was lost.
And all for the want of a horseshoe nail.

As a result of 'inter-being', we are connected not just to clouds, but to a nail in a distant farmhouse, a butterfly in Brazil, and who knows what else. Every part of us is the result of other things, which could be unimaginably far away in both space and time, and seemingly inconsequential.

Since all things in the universe depend on everything else, we are just reflections of what's going on elsewhere. At the same time, it means that the equal and opposite is also true: the universe is just a reflection of us. We contain all the universe in ourselves.

In the Flower Garland Sutra it is written that the Lord of the Universe, Indra, has a net in which there is a jewel at every knot. Each jewel reflects every other jewel. All of them share and mirror something of the others. Tang dynasty monk Fazang, when trying to explain this idea to the Empress Wu, set up a room that he called the Mirror Hall. On every wall were mirrors, and in the centre a candlelit statue of the Buddha, which was reflected endlessly in all directions. In the same way, each of us is reflected in every other jewel in Indra's Net, just as we reflect them.

Modern physics is nearing a similar understanding, with the concept of 'intertwined quanta'. In one of the weirder conclusions of quantum theory, it turns out that if two particles interact at some point, then they are linked forever after, no matter how far they may later travel away from each other. If the spin of particle A goes up, then the spin of particle B must go down, and it has been proved that the information contained in this linkage travels faster than the speed of light.

That's a problem because according to Einstein's theory of relativity, nothing can travel faster than the speed of light. Einstein viewed 'intertwined quanta' with deep suspicion, calling it 'spooky action at a distance'. Nevertheless, while seemingly impossible, 'spooky action at a distance' has been proven again and again in scientific experiments.

Based on what science is now telling us, 'inter-being' is more far-reaching than we ever imagined. With all quanta linked since the Big Bang, when everything was very close together, it means the atoms in our bodies are linked to all the other atoms in existence, even of inconceivably distant universes. Each of us is a microcosm, containing and reflecting the whole.

空不異色

Ku bu i shiki – Emptiness does not differ from the material world

One way to define 'emptiness' might be, quite simply, 'everything changes'. It's the inevitable result of 'inter-being'. In Buddhism this is the principle of *mujo* 無常, often translated as 'impermanence'. That's the idea behind the poetic 'evanescence' infusing Japanese literature and theatre which had so intrigued Marguerite Yourcenar.

The realization that things are in constant flux is expressed in some of humankind's earliest writings. In the fifth century BC, the Greek philosopher Heraclitus famously stated: 'No man ever steps in the same river twice, for it is not the same river and he is not the same man.'

For the ancient Hindus, the never-ending change of all things was represented by the ecstatic dance of Shiva. Impermanence was also Buddha's starting point. Youth and beauty fade, friends and lovers must part, people and objects grow old and disappear. With all things interlinked in the fast-moving currents of the cosmos, nothing can ever stay the same for more than an instant.

The thirteenth-century Japanese epic *The Tale of the Heike* opens with these lines:

The sound of the bell of Gion Shoja echoes with the impermanence of all things. The colour of the *sala* flowers

shows that the great must decline. The proud do not last
long; they are like an evening's dream in the springtime.
The mighty fall in the end; they are just like dust before the
wind.

Wistful reflection about loss and change was a constant theme
in Chinese and Japanese poetry. Japan's earliest poetry anthology, the eighth-century *Man'yoshu*, contains a verse by Otomo
no Yakamochi entitled 'Song of Grief at the Impermanence of
this World'. In it, the poet compares the change of the seasons
and phases of the moon to ageing and the decline of our own
bodies. The idea, which went deeply into Japanese thinking, is
that just as nature is ephemeral, so are we.

This gave rise to a sense of wonder, tinged with sadness,
known in Japanese as *mono-no-aware*. The cult of cherry
blossoms is not so much about the happy week when the
trees are in full bloom, as the sad day when the petals start
to fall.

If the blossoms had always existed, and always would, then
what would be the interest in them? They would be the equiv-
alent of plastic flowers. It's because cherry blossoms last only
for a few days that we find them so poignant.

Mono-no-aware is a poetic approach to what's known nowadays in the West as 'mindfulness'. 'Mindfulness' means keeping
richly aware of each moment, for the very reason that it will
vanish and never come again.

Within the great chaotic flow of life, nothing like us ever
existed before, and we will never come again. Each instant is
to be treasured; and so even a moment without 'mindfulness'
is a terrible waste.

In the words of the fourteenth-century Japanese monk Yoshida Kenko: 'If the dew of Adashino [the western graveyard] were never to fade, if the smoke over Toribeyama [the northern graveyard] never dispersed – if we lived only with that, how could we ever be moved by *mono-no-aware*! The uncertainty of life is what makes it most precious.'

色即是空

Shiki soku ze ku – The material world is itself emptiness

The fabric of time and space appears ever more empty as we explore it from the vantage point of quantum physics. It turns out that the Buddhists stumbled upon a scientific truth as eventful as the Greeks' discovery of the atom. We now know that material objects, at the micro level, do indeed consist of a lot of nothingness. The particles that make them up amount to no more than a buzz of force fields and quantum possibilities. Dr Johnson's foot was not making contact with the actual matter of a stone, but only with a resistant cloud of atomic buzz.

The tiny particles swirling within the buzz are constantly popping into and out of existence. The Tibetan teaching of the *Kalachakra* (the Wheel of Time), which had featured to such striking psychedelic effect in David Kidd's living room, speaks of 'space particles' – tiny monads, or even universes, which are temporarily in a void state between existences.

Meanwhile, it turns out that in quantum physics complete emptiness is also not allowable. There's always the faint possibility that something could occupy even the tiniest space, and so particles take advantage of those possibilities and manifest if only for an infinitesimal instant. Within the emptiness of space, ghostly particles bubble away, filling every quantum niche with 'virtual particle foam'.

In the quantum world, real objects consist of a seething half-empty soup in which virtual particles keep materializing and dematerializing. From the purely physical point of view, the material world does indeed not differ from emptiness, and vice versa.

空即是色

Ku soku ze shiki – Emptiness is itself the material world

One might wonder why we need to dwell on 'emptiness' and 'the material world', and ask if there's anything to be gained by trying to get our heads around this rigmarole. Hakuin speaks for us all when he exclaims in exasperation about these four lines: 'A nice kettle of stew. It's been ruined by dropping in a couple of rat turds.'

The two rat turds are of course 'the material world', and 'emptiness'. The stew was cooking away nicely until those two got dropped in. But if I could speak in defence of emptiness, it seems to me there is at least one good reason for mentioning it.

Emptiness leads to 'equanimity', perhaps the most unique virtue espoused by Buddhism. It's the ability to let go. With equanimity, we calm the turbulent inner waters of the mind, so that external things no longer affect us. The archetype is the blissfully calm face of a statue of the Buddha. You could say that the serene smile of the quietly meditating Buddha is the very symbol of Buddhist enlightenment.

Inside us, desires and passions rage in a constant battle, but discovering the concept of emptiness forges a truce between them. The Dalai Lama calls this 'inner disarmament' and writes about how important it is: 'In all levels of our existence – family life, social life, working life, and political life – inner disarmament is, above all, what humanity needs.'

The Indian mystic Osho translates 'emptiness' as 'nothingness'. According to him: 'Nothingness is the fragrance of the beyond. It is the opening of the heart to the transcendental . . . Man is complete only when he has come to this fragrance, when he has come to this absolute nothingness inside his being, when this nothingness has spread all over him, when he is just a pure sky, unclouded.'

The intoxicating sweetness of nothingness infuses the Heart Sutra from start to finish. Its fragrance arises from equanimity, which in the old Pali canon used in South East Asia is called *upekkha*. Often translated in English as 'non-attachment', it represents a pure and clear-sighted state of mind able to accept that what will be will be.

There's a story about the eleventh-century poet Su Dongpo who sent the following poem to the Zen master Fo-yin:

The eight winds blow, but I am unmoved
I sit straight up on a purple and gold lotus.

The 'eight winds' are praise, ridicule, suffering, happiness, benefit, destruction, gain and loss. Fo-yin sent back a two-word reply: 'Fart, fart.' Furious, Su Dongpo rushed across the Yangtze to the other side of the river where the Master lived and complained loudly about such rudeness.

Fo-yin replied: 'Who was I slandering? You said that you were unmoved by the winds of the eight directions, but just by letting two small farts I've blown you all the way across the Yangtze. And you still say that the winds of the eight directions don't move you?'

On the other hand, when you get close to true *upekkha*, you may find that it's lonely up there in the thin air, far above the world of humankind, all the wrongs and rights, every yes and no. The Zen classic *Blue Cliff Record* records this much-quoted conversation:

> A monk asked Hyaku-Jo, 'What is the most wonderful thing there is?'
> Jo said, 'Sitting alone on a great noble peak.'

You need stamina and oxygen tanks to stay up on that peak for very long, even though the view is total exaltation.

The kanji character that the Chinese and Japanese use for *upekkha* is 捨 *sha*, a vivid word which literally means 'to throw away'. In English, we can express equanimity with two short but rather brutal words: 'So what?' In his book *From A to B, and Back Again*, Andy Warhol uses it as a formula for dispelling all sorrow:

> Sometimes people let the same problem make them miserable for years when they could just say, 'So what.' That's one of my favorite things to say. 'So what.'
> 'My mother didn't love me.' So what.
> 'My husband won't ball me.' So what.
> 'I'm a success but I'm still alone.' So what.

受想行識

Ju so gyo shiki – Sensation, Thought, Action and Consciousness

In the previous four lines, the 'Four Profundities', the sutra has been speaking only of the first of the Five Baskets, *shiki* 色 ('the material world'). Now it goes on to the other four baskets. Typical of a Buddhist list, they're arranged in a sequence, one leading to another. Material objects, as we experience them, give rise to Sensation; which leads to Thought; which triggers Action; culminating in Consciousness. Consciousness is the last and highest of the five baskets. It's also the most troublesome.

In the kabuki play *Dojoji*, the dancing girl holds out a closed fist and then engages the monks in a Buddhist debate. In old male-dominated Asia, a woman shouldn't stand a chance against monks, but it's the celestial maiden versus Shariputra all over again. She challenges the monks to tell her if the bird held in her closed hand is alive or dead. 'If you think it is, it is,' she says.

The monks respond: 'If we think it's not, it's not.' But when she opens her fist, there's no bird, either alive or dead. She wins. She and the monks then recite: *Shiki soku ze ku, ku soku ze shiki* ('The material world is itself emptiness. Emptiness is itself the material world').

While it's presented as just a bit of comedic playacting, the banter in the *Dojoji* debate is based on a koan, one of those impossible questions they assign to students of Zen when they are meditating. One of the most famous koans (by Hakuin) is: 'You know the sound of two hands. What's the sound of one hand?' Another one is: 'The eastern mountain walks on water.'

You can't solve a koan rationally. The answer comes when the mind lets go of its usual concerns, rising to a higher plane. It might be in a sudden flash; or it might come slowly like dawn light creeping in. Koans usually take the form of an enigmatic phrase or a mental riddle, but a koan can be something much larger, a life riddle. An example would be the deafness of Beethoven, which seemed to the composer to be a devastating blow, but which led to his last great masterpieces. Each of us has one or even several 'life koans' that we have to deal with. You wish to start up a company but have no money. You're an ambitious woman but up against a strong glass ceiling in your predominantly male company. You have set out to write a book on the Heart Sutra, but feel inadequate to the task.

'The material world is itself emptiness' and the other lines about the material world being empty and vice versa are a string of koans and negations leading straight down a rabbit hole of confusion. That's where I found myself while I was writing this book – the further I progressed, the less point I could see in any of it. At a dinner party in Kyoto, I happened to meet Hasunuma Ryochoku of Nanzenji Zen Temple. Hearing that he was an authority on the Heart Sutra, I explained my dilemma. 'I feel like I'm mired in quicksand. The more I struggle, the deeper I sink,' I told him. 'Congratulations,' he replied. 'You're almost there!'

亦復如是

Yaku bu nyoze – Are also just like this

After going through each of the Five Baskets, including Consciousness itself, the sutra throws them all out of the window. Just as the material world is nothing but emptiness, the same applies to all the rest.

A key word here is *nyoze* 如是, a translation of the Sanskrit word *evam* – 'like this' or 'such'. 'Just like everything else,' this line says, the other four baskets are also empty. However, as with many other words in the Heart Sutra, *nyoze*, a seemingly bland little particle simply meaning 'such', reveals a sparkling jewel-like interior, rich with significance, when we pick it up and peer into it. In later Buddhism, *nyoze* (*evam*) took on cosmic overtones, and many a book and sermon was written about just this one short word.

The eleventh-century Indian thinker Vajrapani wrote that *evam* is 'the source of 84,000 doctrines and the basis of all marvels'. He valued the word so highly because it points at what lies beyond the apparent emptiness of the world – that is, the sheer 'suchness' of things. It's the wonder of something being just what it is. *Nyoze* is what Zen monks discover when they find cosmic enlightenment in a pointing finger or a sand garden, or in the way they arranged their shoes at the doorway. At that moment, they have seen beyond the realness or non-realness of things to the ineffable 'thusness' of the universe. Mystics see this in their moment of epiphany.

Feeling the 'suchness' can happen with psychedelic drugs, or a supreme meditation, when you feel a blissful union with everything around you, every blade of grass. You're not able to stay at that level all the time, but for a few brief minutes or hours, it's ecstasy. You know that your life has forever changed.

Seeing and fully accepting *nyoze* – that's what it's all about. That said, one should beware of thinking, 'Let's just enjoy the "suchness", and all will be well.' Gilkey was strong in his insistence on how important it is to learn real things about life and how to live it, and not just go into rapture over a good drug high or the splendour of a beautiful garden.

'You have a wonderful feeling,' he said, 'and there were all those wonderful colours and then you say to everybody, "It was so wonderful, don't you understand? I had these marvellous insights; suddenly I realized what life and the world is all about." But then they ask, well, what is life and the world all about, and you have no answer whatsoever – "Oh, it's ineffable." Ineffable is a great word, but it actually means that you're just as dumb as you were before.'

Sad to say, once you've come down from the ecstasy, you're back once again to *gyo* ('practice'). The problem is how to hold on to that feeling of blissful oneness, even as you go about your daily life with all of its pain and annoyances. The Tibetans call this 'equipoise'. In the words of the fifteenth-century Tibetan monk Jamyang Gawai Lodrö: 'One should abide in equipoise on the single taste of the suchness.'

PART 3

The Six Nots

舍利子。	Oh Shariputra!
是諸法空相	All these ways of being are empty appearances.
不生不滅、	Not arising, not extinguished.
不垢不淨、	Not sullied, not pure.
不增不減。	Not increasing, not decreasing.

With a sharp rap on the knuckles, maybe even a Zen smack on the back with a big stick, Kannon brings Shariputra back to focus on emptiness. This time the bodhisattva uses the phrase 'empty appearances'. The emphasis is on illusion – nothing is as it appears to be.

Kannon underscores that with emphatic denial. The three phrases, beginning with 'Not arising, not extinguished' and ending in 'Not increasing, not decreasing', keep repeating in a staccato rat-ta-tat-tat rhythm the syllable *fu* 不, which means 'not'.

'Emptiness', as propounded by the third-century philosopher Nagarjuna, is an expansive, rich concept, a luscious night flower, flush with expanding white petals and an intoxicating if noxious scent. This towering, stinking but mesmerizing corpse-flower had grown from just one tiny seed, which was the word 'not'.

Nagarjiuna maintained that we can't take the truth of anything for granted, even emptiness, for that would make emptiness into a 'thing'. So he said 'not' to everything. In trying to explain the concept of emptiness, Nagarjuna proclaimed the 'Eight Nots', written as 'Eight *Fu*' 八不 (pronounced *Happu* in Japanese). These are:

Not arising, not extinguished.
Not permanent, not transient.
Not one, not the other.
Not coming, not going.

Here in the Heart Sutra we have a set of just six negations, but they're a riff on the same theme:

Not arising, not extinguished.
Not sullied, not pure.
Not increasing, not decreasing.

Nagarjuna not only said 'not', but he also stopped at 'not'. In declaring 'not one, not the other', he denied that you could ever come up with a final answer to anything, and so renounced even the logic that is so dear to Buddhism. Nagarjuna told us what emptiness, wisdom and enlightenment are *not*, but never went on to say what they actually are.

舍利子

Sharishi – Oh Shariputra!

Shariputra is the link between the Buddha, way up there in nirvana, and us way down here.

The Buddha taught the wisdom of *Hannya Haramita* to the bodhisattva Kannon, who passed it on to Shariputra. The tradition is that another disciple, Ananda, compiled Kannon's words into a sutra. But it was the sixth century BC, and the Buddha judged that it was too early for the Perfection of Wisdom to be released to humankind.

Hannya Haramita is an early example of what the Tibetans called 'hidden teachings'. It's believed that sages of earlier eras buried the manuscripts of such secret teachings in caves or at the bottom of lakes, where they would lie for centuries, waiting to be discovered. The later sages who find these hidden manuscripts and bring them into the world are called *tertons*.

The *Hannya Haramita* sutras would have to remain hidden until the world was ready for them. Buddha commanded Ananda to hand the wisdom sutras to the nagas, or water dragons, for safekeeping, and the nagas kept them in their hoard under the sea, like the dragon Fafnir in Norse mythology, guarding his treasure, for seven hundred years.

Finally Nagarjuna, around the year AD 200, got the nagas to release the sutras from their underwater cave. He was thus the first *terton*, or finder of hidden teachings. From Nagarjuna, the

Perfection of Wisdom expanded and multiplied into its many different versions, large, medium and small, right down to the Heart Sutra, found by Xuanzang on his travels five centuries later. The various versions of the Perfection of Wisdom sutras then went west to Tibet, and east to Japan. At each step, masters such as Fazang, Kukai and Hakuin taught the secrets to their disciples, who passed the knowledge on.

This is why Buddhism values lineage so highly. In the subtemples of Zen monasteries in Japan, on the central altar in the abbot's hall, you don't see the Buddha. There's just a statue of the founder of the temple, often with a rather angry expression, maybe holding a stick and looking as if he were about to leap from his chair and strike you. He symbolizes the long chain of teachers and disciples that have kept the flame alive since the very beginning.

I learned about the Heart Sutra for the first time from the Zen monk Urata on the day of the dismantling of David Kidd's palace. And after that there was Tamasaburo in the kabuki theatre, and later the input of many more, including writers I never met, such as the Tibetan monk Geshe Sonam Rinchen and the Japanese calligrapher Kazuaki Tanahashi. I found different inspiration in Yourcenar, and then Gilkey. And now I am putting these words to paper – another link in the chain.

While I was working on this book, a friend asked, 'What's the particular insight about the Heart Sutra that you wish to impart?' I had to think about that for a while. I looked again at the books and articles I had read about the Heart Sutra and saw that they could be sorted into three groups: scholarly – experts combing through ancient texts to figure out the sutra's original intent; philosophical – monks teaching the deep meaning of 'emptiness'; and motivational – inspirational authors telling you how the sutra can change your life.

I realized that my focus belongs in a different category which you could call 'transmission' – that is, passing on what I've learned from others. The one thing I have done all my life is listen to mentors. When I was young, I sat at the feet of people I thought were intriguing. All I wanted to do was to soak up their unpredictable insights, sometimes profound and sometimes playful. Whether it was William Gilkey or Marguerite Yourcenar, I clung on their words, I memorized them, I went home and wrote them down. I even recorded them as they spoke.

As for the Heart Sutra, the monk-magician Fazang from the seventh century and Zen abbot Hakuin from the eighteenth, wrote things that are so striking and even amusing that I can easily feel I'm having the same sort of conversation with them that I used to have with the living mentors at whose feet I sat.

Marguerite Yourcenar, despite our plan to write about the Heart Sutra together, never in fact expected me to carry through with it, or any other writing. Some years after she died, they published posthumously her last journals under the title *Le tour de la prison*, and I found that she had reminisced about me in them. I was touched to read her description of my rural lifestyle in the grounds of an old Shinto shrine. But this was followed, soberingly, by the words: 'He is planning a book that he may never write.'

Now I am writing in an effort to transmit the wisdom that I glimpsed when I talked to, or read the writings of, the people I've admired as gurus. None of them offered a big final answer, but, borrowing the words of Hakuin, each provided pieces of 'small wisdom'.

If I could pass on anything from the many thinkers of the past who have pondered the Heart Sutra, it would be the world of questions this little sutra has inspired. Each question is a shimmering hall showered in gold dust contained within the little room at the top of Maitreya's Tower – expanding to yet more gold-dusted halls, and reflecting them all.

是諸法空相

Ze shoho ku so – All these ways of being are empty appearances

Buddhism was obsessed from the start with 'cause and effect'. But when Buddhist philosophers looked closely at the sequence of events needed to bring about a single human life, they found that an uncountable number of coincidences had to happen in order for any one of us to be born. Our parents had to somehow meet, as did their parents, and their grandparents, back through the ages. And then, down the millennia, everything else had to be going just right. The eighth/ninth-century monk Saicho, who brought Tendai Buddhism from China to Japan describes the chain of coincidences needed for the creation of a single human life as 'like finding a needle in the great sea, or picking up a single thread dangling from a high peak'.

Within the roiling sea of coincidences, you can never separate things you did of your own accord from 'fate' or 'luck'. When you feel you've achieved something, it's sobering to reflect on how much of your success is due to supportive parents, good health, or arbitrary advantages of race and nationality. As well as the job opening that appeared when it did, or the chance meeting with a mentor that changed your destiny.

The way one's life has turned out, the way the world is going – these are the result of chaotic coincidences, out of our control or even our understanding. That is, they are nothing but 'empty appearances'. As Epictetus says in the *Enchiridion*, we are merely actors in a play:

> You are an actor in a drama of such sort as the Author
> chooses – if short, then in a short one; if long, then in a long
> one. If it be his pleasure that you should enact a poor man,
> or a cripple, or a ruler, or a private citizen, see that you act
> it well. For this is your business – to act well the given part,
> but to choose it belongs to another.

不生不滅

Fusho fumetsu – Not arising, not extinguished

The dearth of writings about the Heart Sutra in the early centuries after it first appeared, around A D 400, was noted long ago. Chinese encyclopedias had listed the names of various early translations, but curiously nobody commented on any of these until around A D 700. That's a three-hundred-year gap, during which there was only silence.

It wasn't until the late twentieth century that someone dared to think the unthinkable and state the obvious. It came as a shock to the Buddhist world when the American scholar Jan Nattier, in an article in a Buddhist journal in 1992, managed to overturn thirteen hundred years of accepted knowledge about the Heart Sutra. Through close analysis of texts in Sanskrit and Chinese, Nattier came to the conclusion that the Heart Sutra had not existed in India before Xuanzang.

One by one, she disposed of the earlier translations from 400 to 600 that had featured in the Buddhist encyclopedias, determining that they were either misdated or spurious or otherwise unaccountable. They had never existed. More seriously, when we look at Xuanzang's Sanskrit to better understand the Chinese, we find that the Sanskrit is of no help, and that the Chinese came first. Nattier showed that Xuanzang appeared to have back-translated a Chinese text into Sanskrit, which was then re-imported to India, and grew into the 'long version' now in use in Tibet. In short, Xuanzang may have made it all up.

But we don't know for sure. Some say it could have been crafted by the sick monk who gave it to Xuanzang when he was travelling in southern China in his youth. Maybe it had been floating around for a while in the border regions of India and China, and the sick monk acquired it from who-knows-where. Nattier figured out that most of the sutra derives from an earlier text by the fourth-century translator Kumarajiva. Whoever compiled the Heart Sutra – whether it was the sick monk on the Silk Road, or Xuanzang himself – apparently lifted a stretch of Kumarajiva's writing, and added a suitable beginning and ending.

Xuanzang's translation – or creation – of the Heart Sutra could be seen as the discovery of a 'hidden teaching'. Xuanzang was a *terton* treasure seeker, as Nagarjuna had been before him. In some sense, the Heart Sutra is itself a mystical lake or cave in which hidden teachings lie buried and hidden, waiting for *tertons* to come and discover them. Once we start peeking into the nooks and crannies of the sutra, we're all *tertons* on a treasure hunt.

In any case, the trail leads to Xuanzang and stops dead in suspicious circumstances. Other scholars have disputed Nattier's findings, but their arguments have not been conclusive. All that can be said is that the world's greatest work on truth and wisdom has dubious origins. It's a closed loop. The sutra had neither a beginning nor an end; it neither arose, nor has it been extinguished.

不垢不浄

Fuku fujo – Not sullied, not pure

Purity of soul is an idea dear to ancient Chinese thinkers. Long before Buddhism reached China, the Confucianist philosopher Mencius, from the third/fourth century BC, believed strongly in our innate good nature. 'People's goodness is like water's tendency to flow down,' he said. 'You can splash it as high as your forehead, or push it to the top of a mountain, but is that really in the nature of water?'

Ancient Indian philosophers did not dwell so much on purity of the soul, because they thought the point was to rise above the soul to something higher. However, there was one group that talked about 'purity', and they were the 'Mind Only' school whose teachings Xuanzang brought to China.

The idea is that we bear within us already the pure nature of a buddha. All we need to do is to wipe the dust off the mirror of the soul, and presto, buddhahood is already there. They called this *bodhicitta* ('buddha nature' or 'buddha heart'), which the Dalai Lama defines as 'the clear-light nature of the mind'. He goes on to say: 'This naturally abiding Buddha nature is known also as *natural nirvana*, or natural liberation, for it exists naturally in all of us.'

This seed of 'purity', falling in China on the rich soil prepared by Mencius and his followers, grew into a mighty tree, one of whose branches was Zen. In a sense, the entire thrust of Zen is to get back to that state of 'natural nirvana' which we have in us to start with, but have lost along the way. Being pure to begin with, our buddha nature can never be sullied; and there was also never any need to purify it. Which of course begs the question of how all the dust got on to the mirror. In the words of the seventh-century Zen patriarch Huineng:

Basically we have not a single thing –
Where could any dust be attracted?

In the prophecies underpinning the establishment of Oomoto in the 1890s, it was stated that the leader would always be a woman, just as in early Shinto, where it was via female shamans that the divine word had been passed down. In our time, during the 1970s and 1980s, the third leader was Madame Deguchi Naohi, whom David called 'the Mother Goddess'. Madame Naohi visited David's home in Ashiya one day, and gave him a calligraphic plaque by her father Onisaburo, the charismatic genius behind the founding of Oomoto.

Written in old-style cursive calligraphy, it was not easy to decipher, but finally we figured it out. It read, *Senshin no gyo*「洗心の行」, which means 'the work of cleansing the heart'.

'And dirty work it is, too,' said David.

不增不減

Fuzo fugen – Not increasing, not decreasing

The Tibetans refer to the three lines featuring *fu* (not) as the 'Three Doors of Liberation'. Leaving aside the first two for the moment, this line ('Not increasing, not decreasing') marks the final stage, known as the 'Door of Wishlessness'.

'Wishlessness' describes the mind of a bodhisattva, who seeks no particular outcome and so is neither especially happy when things turn out well, nor sad when they don't. Increase and decrease mean nothing to him. He can never be disappointed. Or rather, he's used to being disappointed and doesn't really mind. As Buddhist scholar Karl Brunnhölzl remarks: 'We could say that the Buddhist path is simply one disappointment after the other – the only good thing is that enlightenment is the last one.'

'Not increasing, not decreasing' is one of the many lines in the Heart Sutra in which a pair of opposites negate each other. In Zen, all the 'nots' of the Heart Sutra are summed up in the term *funi* 不二, or 'not-two'. It means non-duality, refusing to categorize things as good or bad, us or them, right or wrong.

'Not-two' features as a koan in the Zen classic *Blue Cliff Record*. The story refers to the time that the wise layman Vimalakirti bested the bodhisattva of wisdom, Manjusri, in a debate. Vimalakirti, although not a monk, was so ruthlessly clever that he had outsmarted all the other bodhisattvas, one after another. So when he fell ill, they all refused to go to visit him, fearing that he would once again embarrass them. Finally, the Buddha ordered Manjusri to go, and he agreed. No sooner had Manjusri arrived at the old man's bedside than Vimalakirti inquired of him, 'What is the Bodhisattva's Gate to "Not-Two"?'

Manjusri replied, 'There are no words, no preaching, no talking, no consciousness. It is beyond all debate. That is entering the Gate to "Not-Two".' Then Manjusri asked Vimalakirti for his view. Vimalakirti said nothing. Manjusri lost because he had tried to use words to describe the wordless.

'The silence of Vimalakirti is like thunder' goes the saying. Silence was a favourite strategy of the Buddha. When asked whether the world is eternal or not, or whether the self is identical to the body, or whether an enlightened being survives death – he responded with silence.

PART 4

No Eyes, Ears, Nose, Tongue, Body or Mind

是故空中、	Therefore, within this emptiness
無色、	There is no material world.
無受・想・行・識。	There is no Sensation, Thought, Action or Consciousness.
無眼・耳・鼻・舌・身・意、	No eyes, ears, nose, tongue, body or mind.
無色・声・香・味・触・法。	No colour, sound, scent, taste, touch or *dharmas*.

These lines are full of the word *mu* 無, meaning 'no'. *Mu* ties in with *fu* 不, which featured in the 'Six Nots' in the section just before this, but whereas *fu* means 'not' in the sense of 'not to *do* something', *mu* means 'not to *be* something'.

Even stronger than *fu*, *mu* is denial, negative, *non*, *nyet*. It's Don Giovanni shouting 'No!' again and again, when asked to repent or be sent to hell, and continuing to bellow 'No!' even as the devils drag him down to a fiery end. It's King Lear raging with grief at his daughter's death: 'Never, never, never, never, never!'

From here on, the sutra takes up each aspect of how we view and live in the world, one at a time, and negates them all. This may be the most 'negating' piece of writing in human history. Following the six *fu* that came just before it, the word *mu* is repeated nineteen times like a relentless drum beat. It rejects, refuses, renounces, repeals, repudiates and refutes.

These lines flesh out – one could say, shout out – the bodhisattva Kannon's realization at the opening of the sutra that 'the Five Baskets are all empty'. Here he blasts into our minds the realization of just how totally empty the baskets are.

We begin with the first of the Five Baskets, 'the material world'. Our intense involvement with it is the root of all our other illusions. Here, the material world is again expressed by the word *shiki* 色, shimmering with the nuances of its original meaning of 'sex' or 'colour'. The sutra turns out the lights and shuts down the music, stating simply and somberly: 'There is no material world.'

The next lines go on to cut away the means by which we apprehend reality, including the sense organs (eyes, nose, etc.) and the senses associated with them: 'colour' (standing for sight), sound and so forth. All these things are illusions. Kukai calls this section 'Cutting Off' and he writes: 'The sharp sword of Manjusri, wielding the Eight *Fu*, cuts off falsely discriminating thoughts.'

Fu and *mu* are the whoosh of Manjusri's flaming Sword of Wisdom as it swoops down, slicing through everything we depend upon.

是故

Ze ko – Therefore

The word 'therefore' 故 appears several times in the Heart Sutra, and reminds us that Buddhism is all about debate. Lists, proving things, QED.

Statues of the Buddha and bodhisattvas often show them holding their hands and fingers in distinctive symbolic gestures known as *mudra*. In the *mudra* of 'Earth Witness', widespread in Thailand and Myanmar, the Buddha is shown with one hand reaching downwards, 'touching the earth', in witness to the truth. In another common *mudra* he appears with one hand upraised, first finger touching the thumb. In this *mudra*, called 'Argumentation' or 'Teaching', he's making a point, as Shakyamuni did in his sermons. He is saying, 'And therefore . . .'

Many volumes have been written detailing the nuances of *ku* 空 ('emptiness') and *mu* 無 ('nothingness'), not to mention the fine points of the Buddhist lists. True to the love of reasoned debate, *mu* negations appear one after another in the order of cause and effect, step by step. First the sutra goes through the list of the Six Sense Organs (which, in addition to eyes, ears and so on, includes the mind), and after that, the list of our responses to the senses. The Buddhist debaters took very seriously the proper use – and order – of words.

In the early days, when David Kidd, Gilkey and I were just beginning our involvement with Oomoto, we found that some of the English-language publications had a rather strident tone.

Part of Gilkey's job as editor was to help smooth those rough edges. One day we came across a line that said: 'We must sweep away and stamp out the enemies of divine love!'

'I should think,' David dryly remarked, 'that you would stamp first and sweep later.'

空中

Ku chu – Within this emptiness

Readers of the Heart Sutra have long puzzled over Nagarjuna's 'Two Truths', by which things are to be seen from one side as real and existent, and from the other side as impermanent and non-existent. Fazang sums it up in four lines of super-succinct classical Chinese:

不空之空、	The emptiness that is not empty –
空而不斷。	Although it's empty, it will not cease.
不有之有、	The existence that does not exist –
有而非常。	Although it exists, it will not endure.

Let's pause and take this slowly. 'The emptiness that is not empty' means emptiness that's very real, like the buzz of particles in the stone that came into contact with Dr Johnson's foot. It may be just a buzz, but it stopped his foot.

'Although it's empty, it will not cease' indicates that the unruly impermanence of things is always there and we have to deal with it. There's another verse by Otomo no Yakamochi in the *Man'yoshu* that states: 'As sad and miserable as I feel about the world, I am not a bird that could just fly away.' We are stuck here; we have to live within the flux and flow.

'Although it exists, it will not endure' reminds us that, however seriously we may take our duties in this material world, our affairs are in the end nothing but 'an evening's dream in

109

the springtime', an illusion. Fazang's shape-shifting phrases sum up the quandary of life in a world that's real on the one hand and empty on the other. We try to accomplish something on this earth; but nothing lasts, and nothing that we do has any absolute value. As Geshe Sonam Rinchen says: 'A Bodhisattva is one who heroically faces and bears the hardship of contemplating the two truths again and again.'

With paradoxical phrases such as Fazang's 'The emptiness that is not empty' one has to take care not to descend into a sort of clichéd 'Heart Sutra-speak'. Around the time Yourcenar and I were contemplating writing our book, I went to Rome, where I had an introduction to Gore Vidal. After we'd talked for a bit, he asked me what I was working on, and, flattered by the attention from the great writer, I discoursed at some length about the paradoxes of the Heart Sutra. In those days I always carried ink, brush and paper with me, and asked people I met to write calligraphy for me. So I made the same request of Gore Vidal. 'Here's some Heart Sutra for you,' Vidal said, and brushed, in English: 'Nothing is no Thing.'

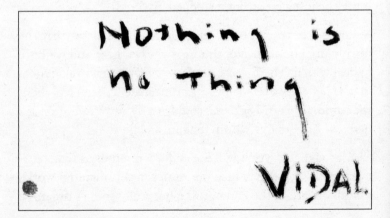

It reads like it might be something profound, but of course it's completely meaningless, and Vidal knew that. It's a parody. Vidal was laughing at me and my Heart Sutra paradoxes. I later had the piece mounted as a hanging scroll, and I put it up sometimes to remind me of how silly all this can sound.

無色

Mu shiki – There is no material world

Whatever the 'material world' may be, it's not what we think it is. That's the point of many Zen sayings. We can't touch or see atoms and electrical forces. We simply have no way to truly experience reality. Our senses show us only something approximate, or even misleading. What we see and believe to be real is nothing but a mental construct.

In the old days at David Kidd's palace in Ashiya, we used to gather in the evening on the moon-viewing platform overlooking the garden at the back of David's bedroom. One chilly November night, garden designer Masaaki was there, and he noticed the strange blooming of cherry blossoms out of season.

'Could that possibly be a cherry tree?' asked Masaaki.

'Yes,' replied David.

'I can see cherry blossoms!' said Masaaki.

'Well,' said David, 'it's just like Persian carpets. You're seeing a pattern that isn't there. Actually, you're looking at bug-eaten leaves, and the spaces look like flowers.'

無受想行

Mu ju so gyo – There is no Sensation, Thought, Action

Because there is no material world, at least as we usually understand it, the other four baskets – which are all derived from our experience of the material world – don't exist either.

From here on, the sutra embarks on a type of Buddhist logic called the 'Vajra Sliver'. A *vajra* 金剛 is a sceptre-like implement tapered at each end. The tips may be rounded or sharp; sometimes ribbed sections open up and then converge at the top and bottom – resembling magnetic lines drawn to north and south poles. At other times, the *vajra* may be very simple, consisting of just a rod ending in two sharp points. Whichever form it takes, the *vajra* is a symbol of spiritual power, related to the Sword of Wisdom, but a weapon of even greater strength. You often see images of bodhisattvas holding *vajras*, or a *vajra* displayed on Esoteric Buddhist altars in Japan. The *vajra* is as forceful as a thunderbolt and hard as a diamond.

A *vajra* is indestructible, yet it has the power to destroy everything else. When you use the *Vajra* Sliver, you cut through things to take a closer look at their causes, what the Buddhists call karma. You slice away what is not essential, or dependent on something else. If you keep chopping at the karma long enough, you eventually find that no one cause can explain the existence of anything.

In the West, 'Occam's razor' embodies something similar. The fourteenth-century theologian William of Ockham (or Occam) is said to have declared: *'Entia non sunt multiplicanda sine necessitate'* ('Entities should not be multiplied without necessity'). Applying this principle (his 'razor', as it was termed later), Ockham and others after him proceeded to pare away layers of Christian dogma, getting dangerously close to God himself. Because none of what they had removed was strictly necessary.

Physical objects, and the ways in which we sense and think about them, are all inter-dependent, random, ephemeral. The diamond-hard *vajra* has cut right through, leaving nothing, or maybe just a bit of diamond dust, behind.

識

Shiki – Or Consciousness

David Kidd owned a shiny black Cadillac of the wide-finned 1960s type, in which he used to glide through downtown Osaka. One time I was riding with him, and a policeman stopped the car after it went through a red light. David rolled down the window, and the policeman started asking questions, his name, address, and other details. And then, 'How old are you?' In a sinister voice like Vincent Price's rumbling from a tomb, David proclaimed, 'Five thousand years.' Smiling nervously, the policeman waved us on.

Reincarnation over many lifetimes is a reassuring idea, but not a feasible belief for many people today. As Buddhist scholar-blogger Jayarava writes: 'The history of Buddhist ideas is dominated by the problem of continuity [after death]: too much and it starts to look like a soul, too little and karma cannot work . . . Physics, it turns out, says that beyond any reasonable doubt there is and can be no personal post-mortem continuity.'

'Consciousness' is the soul. The sutra says: 'No such thing.' This should not come as a surprise, because, from the beginning, Shakyamuni had denied the existence of a permanent soul. That created endless confusion because people believed in the workings of rebirth and karma, a system whereby the soul was reborn again and again in a process of working its way up the spiritual ladder. So the concept of the soul kept creeping back in.

But maybe there is 'reasonable doubt'. Buddhist theorist Alan Wallace points out that so far science has failed to make any headway in understanding what consciousness actually is. So it remains possible that consciousness is distinct from the physical functions of the brain and does not cease at death. We can say that the jury is still out.

Meanwhile, if there is no soul to reincarnate for five thousand years, we're up against the classic 'Atheist's Dilemma'. It's how to answer the question of one of David Kidd's more unsavoury friends, 'Finky Frank', who was in the habit of passing bad cheques and defrauding people in various ways. One day Frank asked of Gilkey, with regard to committing yet another scam, 'Why should I make any sacrifices for anybody?'

Gilkey's reply to Frank boiled down to what I would call 'the Law of Advance'. His approach was that just as the universe obeys laws of entropy and evolution that flow in a forward direction invariably with time, the human spirit also advances. *Bodhicitta* ('buddha heart' or 'buddha nature'), which we've met earlier, is built into the very fabric of the cosmos. The desire to be wise and good is not optional. As with entropy, you can try to escape its effects, but only temporarily and at ever-increasing cost. Advance we must, or suffer.

Back in the early 1990s, I recorded hours of Gilkey's and my talks about spiritualist lore, and among those recordings I find this:

G: Jesus said, 'Lay not up riches for yourself on earth, but riches in heaven where moth and "something,

something" do not corrupt.' Now, we know what those riches are going to be. The knowledge of spiritual advance really spells out the consequences of selfishness.

A: So it's a more sophisticated version of morality? The fear of hellfire has been polished a little bit.

G: How else can you keep your horse from going in the wrong direction?

Jayarava declares: 'The onus is on humans to both reward and punish more assiduously, and to think very carefully about what constitutes good and evil, because the universe is not going to square things up after death.'

Gilkey believed in the soul; Jayarava dismisses it. But they both came to a similar conclusion, which is that, immortal soul or not, we still have to try to do the right thing. David Kidd's attitude was that anything goes, so long as it's amusing. He used to say: 'If you must laugh, you should have something really worthwhile to laugh about. Like your Immortal Soul.'

無眼

Mu gen – No eyes

The eyes, ears, nose and so on are the Six Sense Organs, which includes the mind as well as the usual five sense organs. The sutra denies all of them.

The thing is, after you have said, 'There is no X,' the fatal word 'X' has been spoken and you can't ignore it. It is like when someone says, 'It's not that I hate apples . . .' You immediately suspect that in fact she does hate apples. The sutra, even as it goes out of its way to deny them, has conjured eyes, ears, nose, tongue, body and mind.

To Occam's Razor and Fazang's Mirror Hall, I would like to add a lesser-known principle, 'McAllister's Sniff'. My friend Dave McAllister, who worked on a farm in rural Pennsylvania, described how it was when he had to carry dead chickens and other animal carcasses to the disposal pit. You hold your breath as you approach because you know how horrible the smell is going to be. But at the last minute, just at the brim of the pit, you can't help but take one little sniff.

This is the point in the sutra where we give in and take a sniff of our mortal selves. We thought we would be aiming at high and noble ideas, but now we are suddenly reminded of our gross physicality. Starting with eyes, and then on to ears, nose, tongue and our bodies with their veins and internal organs and excretions.

This is the 'person' that the doctor sees on the operating table, a conglomeration of sinews and hormones and DNA. Eyes are not things that just magically see. They need the right nerves and fluids to function harmoniously, and almost all those things are completely out of our control.

耳鼻舌身

Ni bi ze shin – No ears, nose, tongue, body

Our eyes, ears, nose, tongue and body are fleshy constructs, far from anything you might think of as intelligent or spiritual, made of stuff that ages and decays. We only see a narrow range of light; we hear and smell less well than dogs. Our senses are utterly inadequate for experiencing the true nature of reality.

The limited senses we do enjoy, don't belong to us for long, and will be taken away. In the *Enchiridion*, there are things that are 'in our power', according to Epictetus, and things that are 'not in our power', and the mind is the last and only thing that is in our power. But even the mind, vulnerable to chemical imbalances, and stricken down finally by age, is not in the end truly in our power.

Shakespeare, as part of the 'All the world's a stage' speech from *As You Like It*, echoes the Heart Sutra when he writes:

. . . Last scene of all,
That ends this strange eventful history,
Is second childishness and mere oblivion,
Sans teeth, sans eyes, sans taste, sans everything.

意

I – Or mind

Two words that we translate in English as 'mind' appear in the sutra. The earlier one, *shiki* 識, which we came across two lines ago, means consciousness in general and, in particular, the soul. This one, *i* 意 (pronounced *ee* as in 'teeth'), means our personal desires, dreams and thoughts – that is, the ego. It's the ego that clings and is lost in *samsara*, the sea of sorrow.

The Indian guru Osho, in his talks about the Heart Sutra, tells a tale about a yogi who agreed to remain under the earth for a year, meditating, in exchange for the king's finest horse:

> But in the course of the year the kingdom was overthrown and nobody remembered to dig up the yogi. About ten years later someone remembered: 'What happened to the yogi?' The king sent a few people to find out. The yogi was dug up; he was still in his deep trance. A previously-agreed-to mantra was whispered in his ear and he was roused, and the first thing he said was, 'Where is my horse?'

Thus do even the great sages cling to their egos. Osho concludes: 'The whole process of The Heart Sutra will make it clear to you that the ego is the only thing that doesn't exist – the only thing that doesn't exist! Everything else is real.'

And yet the ego does, of course, exist. 'We are constantly being admonished to fight our egos,' said Gilkey. 'People take this to mean they should sit in meditation and disapprove of themselves in some way. But just doing what is asked of you is hard enough on the poor ego. Don't worry so much about your ego and just get on with your job.'

David Kidd was not one to dismiss his ego easily. 'I gave my ego up to God,' he pronounced, 'and He gave it back to me. He said, "You need this more than I do." '

無色

Mu shiki – No colour

Here *shiki* 色, used elsewhere in the sutra to mean the 'material world', appears in its usual sense of 'colour'. It stands for 'sight' in general – that is, 'everything we can see with our eyes'. This and the next few lines refer to the objects of our sense organs – what the ears hear, the nose smells, up to what the mind perceives. Since the sense organs were denied earlier, the sutra now denies the contents of what they have sensed.

This brings us to art. At the time I met Gilkey, I was besotted by David Kidd and the transcendent beauties of his shining palace. As David swept open the silver doors to the inner rooms, you felt you had entered a portal right back to Ming China. Oomoto, the Shinto foundation where I used to work, with its emphasis on calligraphy, Noh drama and the tea ceremony, only reinforced our belief that art is sublime.

One night at David's palace, he displayed four fine art objects on wooden stands. David pointed out that the educated elite of China were the very first in the world to rise above religion. Confucius had said early on, 'Respect gods and spirits, but keep them at a distance', and in later centuries the literati remained aloof from both Buddhism and Daoism. 'All they had left to believe in was art,' said David, 'and so they raised it up on stands. That's why practically every Chinese art work has a stand, whether it's a ceramic bowl or a carved jade.'

At Oomoto, with David as our high priest, we raised art high on the altar. Then Gilkey arrived. Looking back on it, it was the appearance of Manjusri on our doorstep. None of us imagined that Manjusri, always portrayed as a cute, boyish figure, would appear in the guise of this balding, portly old man. Gilkey advocated a number of health regimens, which included consuming cloves of honeyed garlic, and dabbing his skin with vinegar. It lent him a peculiar odour, far from the heavenly incense one would have expected from Manjusri. Nor from his homey Oklahoma twang would we have expected to hear words divine. But we learned over time that Gilkey wielded a sword as sharp as Manjusri's.

David, who had known Gilkey from his old days in Beijing in the 1940s, brought him to Oomoto to edit our English-language publications. Soon after Gilkey's arrival, David asked him to participate in Oomoto's Seminar of Traditional Japanese Arts. However, in just two days, Gilkey was standing in the office begging David to please be relieved from participation in the tea ceremony. As Gilkey walked out, David commented to me, 'There goes a man who truly *hates* the traditional Japanese arts!'

And it was true. Gilkey looked down on all arts, and also artists and art collectors, for their snobbism and self-centredness. This despite the fact that Gilkey was himself a musical artist. He had studied music at Harvard and Juilliard, and had gone on to build a career as a concert pianist in India and China. He kept an upright piano in his little house in Kameoka, and played haunting renditions of Brahms and Mompou for his visitors. Even so, he never held his music up as an important achievement. His low view of the arts came as a shock to me because I had until then seen art as the highest level of spirituality.

For Gilkey, the thing that mattered was whether a person was kind and doing his or her best to help others. If they created art, or appreciated it, this was much lower on the spiritual scale. If they were a great collector or owner of art, that was even less admirable, and might even point to some unpleasant personality flaws.

That was a very useful lesson, especially for someone in the circle of the brilliant David Kidd. In later years, I was grateful to Gilkey for having shown me another way. Or, at least, for trying. He never did break my addiction to beautiful things, and I'm still an obsessive collector of Asian art, forever striving to recreate David's enchanted living room. But at least I know, as Gilkey taught me, that while appreciating art might be joyful, it doesn't make me spiritual.

声香

Sho ko – [No] sound, scent

While the Heart Sutra denies sensual pleasures, art is still a big part of what it is to be human, and so the question remains of how to fit it in.

Tamasaburo told me once that when he is on stage, and he can sense that he has captured the audience, and swept them up to his level of supernal beauty, he feels he has become a *miko*, a shamaness of old. As he lifts his hands and poses triumphantly at the finale, the divine *miko* is carrying all those seated in the theatre into another dimension. The artist is a shamaness, rending the veil, so we can see the wonder on the other side. Art, and not just human art, but the glories of nature, takes us out of the cold empty Heart Sutra world.

Jesus, Confucius and Buddha had little to say about art. Yet our most primitive ancestors of tens of thousands of years ago felt driven to carve a Venus of Willendorf, or paint deer on cave walls. Even the Neanderthals made art, painting caves with abstract designs, it was recently discovered, so it appears that art precedes even what it means to be human. It goes back to what it means to be alive.

Darwin, as he pondered the theory of evolution, was much troubled by the peacock's lavish tail feathers, which, heavy and cumbersome, could have no possible advantage in 'natural selection'. After looking at other species, he came to the conclusion that animals (usually it's the females) often select their mates by sheer beauty. It might be a songbird choosing the loveliest song, or a crane preferring the most charming mating-dance footwork, or a female puffer fish opting for the most intricate pattern carved by a male fish with his fins in the sea-floor sand. Recent research has shown that a sense of beauty is hardwired into animals' brains, even those of tiny frogs, and is one of the most powerful drivers of evolution. Darwin called this 'a taste for the beautiful'.

Zen abbots, while they carry on about emptiness, love their elegant temple halls and sand gardens. Art is all around them. In China, the Heart Sutra, at a very early stage – just two decades after its first appearance – became intimately connected with one particular art form: calligraphy. For many people, the sutra is almost synonymous with the act of brushing it beautifully.

Nonetheless, aesthetics and spiritual advance don't seem to mix well, just as, in the realm of physics, no one has yet managed to come up with a 'Grand Unified Theory' to reconcile Einstein's relativity with quantum physics. The closest we have come to a grand theory that unifies art and wisdom might be the attempt by Socrates in the *Symposium* in which he argues that we begin with a love of the beauty of the human body, and progress from that to loving moral quality. Socrates stands in surprising agreement with Darwin in that the starting point is physical beauty of people and animals. This also brings sex nicely into the mix.

Art gives expression, in a way that no one has ever been able to explain or justify, to something deep in the universe and in ourselves. It leaps above and beyond the implacable emptiness.

味触

Mi soku – [No] taste, touch

No taste or touch – more sensual pleasures denied. Looking again at my Gilkey conversations:

G: People tend to run away with art. It's the light, the sound, the sweep of the feelings. I think that any time people are carried away it's a most unedifying spectacle. Actually, you can stand and look down into a toilet full of teeming maggots and have just as genuine a spiritual experience as you can listening to the music of Beethoven.

A: Beethoven's late quartets do remind me just a teensy bit of teeming maggots. Anyway, if maggots are just as good as a great work of art, are we not back to the idea that the world is all a snare and a delusion, and you must turn your back on it?

G: No, I think it was an understanding of this around which a fanatical doctrine formed, and they ended up believing that if you have sex you're damned and all that sort of thing. I do not believe that there is all that much difference between a man looking at the female figure and getting a strong aesthetic reaction to it, and a lady walking into a garden and making over the lovely blossoms she sees there. All of these are the pleasures of the flesh.

A: The beauties of the world are just 'pleasures of the flesh'?

G: They exist as intuitions of what we are on our way to attaining. They keep harping from the other side too, about how much more beautiful their music is, and how much more glorious their paintings are. So the pleasure that we get out of sunsets and symphonies is just a peek at coming attractions. Or even the taste of a good guacamole.

A: I don't see how they can have anything that good.

法

Ho – Or *dharmas*

Ho 法, literally meaning 'law', is the word the early Chinese translators chose for *dharma*. One of the most commonly used and yet difficult of all Buddhist concepts, *dharmas* refer to the laws of the universe, or to all mental and physical phenomena generally. The most basic meaning is simply 'nature'.

Applied to a particular object or activity, *dharmas* are the rules by which it functions. The *dharmas* of roses would be all the things that make them unique and cause them to exist, such as rose DNA, the shape of rose petals, their perfume, and also the places where roses bloom, and the pleasure they bring to people. *Dharmas* are the 'rhyme and reason' of things. If light is what our eyes sense, then *dharmas* are what our minds sense.

Since *dharmas* are the properly functioning laws of the universe, the ideal *dharmas* are seen to be the teachings of the Buddha. It's common to refer to these collectively as 'the *Dharma*' with a capital D. So Buddhists everywhere pay homage to the 'Three Gems': the Buddha, the *Dharma* (the teachings) and the *Sangha* (the community).

Here the sutra denies all *dharmas*, since we have arrived at them via our inadequate senses and shallow minds. We hear much from Buddhist writers about how you should not be too rational. Woncheuk, Xuanzang's foremost Korean disciple, stressed that 'discrimination' (judging right and wrong, true and false, etc.) leads us to misunderstand the *dharmas*. He wrote:

> With mind discriminating, all *dharmas* are erroneous.
> With mind not discriminating, *dharmas* are all correct.

In other words, the more we think about these things, the more we miss the mark. It's tempting to let go of our probing minds, and float away in the balmy pond of meditation. But Hakuin, writing in *Poison Words on the Heart Sutra*, brings us back down to earth: 'Well, I have eyes and ears,' he huffs. 'And a nose, tongue, body, and mind. Forms, sounds, smells, tastes, touch, and *dharmas* do exist!'

The way forward is to use our intelligence. That's how we can reach a greater wisdom and rise to a higher plane. The Dalai Lama writes: 'Our intelligence gives us the ability to remember the past, and it allows us to envision possibilities for the future – both good ones and bad . . . Ultimately the unhappiness created by human intelligence can only be alleviated by intelligence itself.'

Woncheuk argues that the mind should not discriminate, whereas the Dalai Lama insists that we must use our intelligence. The trouble is that a concept like 'The material world is the same as emptiness' defies rational thought, and yet as human beings we have a duty to use our minds.

How much should you think, or try not to think? This is one of the biggest conundrums of Buddhism.

PART 5

No Ageing and No Death

無眼界、	There is no world of sight,
乃至、無意識界。	And the same for the rest; there is no world of consciousness.
無無明 、	There is no ignorance.
亦無無明尽。	And, likewise, there is no end to ignorance.
乃至、無老死、	And the same for the rest; there is no ageing and death.
亦無老死尽。	Likewise, there is no end to ageing and death.

The sutra continues in denial mode, with the word *mu* repeated again and again, a series of 'nos' denying first one thing, and then denying the denial!

One of the weird and wonderful creations of Buddhist logic was the so-called 'tetralemma'. Derived from a Sanskrit word meaning 'four corners', a tetralemma is a 'proof with four corners', or four sub-arguments, and Nagarjuna, master of paradoxes, pioneered the use of it. Buddhist scholar Jan Westerhoff outlines how it works:

There is P
There is not-P
There is P and not-P
There is neither P nor not-P

Nagarjuna would go through and deny all four of these statements. He would show that *none* of them were true. Just replace 'P and not-P' with 'the material world and emptiness' or 'ignorance and no end to ignorance', and we get the familiar tetralemma-like rhythm of the Heart Sutra.

Many have wrestled with the tetralemma in order to try to explain how these contradictions could work logically. How could all four statements be false? One solution is that we're dealing with 'pre-supposition failure' – that is, we have asked the wrong question. For example, if you ask, 'Is the number three yellow or not?' you have pre-supposed something about the number three that's not relevant.

In classical Western thinking, 'There is P and not-P' just can't be true. According to the 'law of excluded middle', the cornerstone of logic ever since Aristotle, for any proposition, either that proposition or its negation is true. Without it, all science and mathematics – maybe the universe itself – would disappear. So when something bizarre turns up in logic, we naturally suspect 'pre-supposition failure'. If we just cleared up our categories, the problem would go away.

But there is at least one significant exception in which the statements 'There is P and not-P' and 'There is neither P nor not-P' are both true and false at the same time, right on the face of it. Aristotle, the very father of Western logic, recognized that. It is the Future.

In modern physics, this is illustrated by the paradox of 'Schrödinger's cat'. In 1935, Austrian physicist Erwin Schrödinger did a 'thought experiment' in which he imagined a cat hidden in a closed box. If one atom of a tiny piece of radioactive matter contained in the box randomly decayed, a vial of poison would break and the cat would die. If not, then the cat would live. According to the peculiar predictions of quantum theory, the atom could be seen as intact or decayed at the same time – and so the cat could be both alive and dead at the same time. We wouldn't know which until we opened the box to see.

It's an updated, scientific version of the debate between the dancing girl and the monks in the kabuki play *Dojoji*, when she holds out her closed hand and asks if the bird in it is alive or dead. Schrödinger invented his cat in a box in order to show the absurdity of quantum theory when applied to real-life objects larger than atomic nuclei – a paradox that can't be true. But later experiments and theory have shown that this is the way reality works. It's preposterous, and it makes no sense, but laboratory results have proven again and again that nuclei can be intact and decayed at the same time; and quantum theory has expanded this uncertainty on a larger and larger scale.

In any case, from a quantum theory point of view, the cat really is both alive and dead at the same time, so long as information about its life or death doesn't affect us in one way or another. As soon as it does, we know for sure. We're back to Aristotle's Future, about which nothing logical can be said.

From the next tiny quantum instant after 'now', until the end of the universe, all things are both true and false, all the cats are both alive and dead. The tetralemma applies to everything.

無眼界

Mu genkai – There is no world of sight

This line denies the 'world of sight' – that is, everything that we have learned through our eyes. The most concentrated *mu* section of the Heart Sutra starts here. The following lines feature a mind-numbing sequence of *mu* followed by yet more *mu*.

Mu is cosmic nothingness, sheer denial. In the thirteenth-century Chinese work *The Gateless Barrier*, a celebrated list of Zen koans, the *Mu Koan* comes first, before all the others. It goes like this:

> A monk asked Joshu, 'Does a dog have a Buddha nature or not?' Joshu answered, '*Mu!*'

The author of *The Gateless Barrier*, Wumen Huikai, spent six years thinking about *mu* before he understood it. In his commentary on the koan, he says:

> Make your whole body a mass of doubt, and with your 360 bones and joints and your 84,000 hair follicles, concentrate on this one word *Mu*. Day and night, keep digging into it. Don't consider it to be nothingness. Don't think in terms of 'has' or 'has not.' It is like swallowing a red-hot iron ball. You try to vomit it out, but you cannot.

Mu is the ache of the great emptiness. However much you think about it, you can't spit it out.

As I was writing this book, a strange thing happened to me in Kyoto. I was showing some visitors around my favourite garden of Daisen-in, a sub-temple of the big Zen complex of Daitokuji. Ozeki Soen, the Abbot of Daisen-in, is a talkative Zen eccentric, usually found seated near the entrance, at a desk piled high with books and calligraphies that he sells to visitors. As soon as he spots me, he starts bantering with me about this and that.

This time we had our usual chat and then my friends and I prepared to depart. But as we were putting on our shoes at the entrance to Daisen-in, I found that the old abbot had walked out to the front of the temple with us. He gestured me to follow him, away from my friends. There was something he wanted to say.

'You know, in Zen, we always talk about *ku* ('emptiness') and *mu* ('nothingness'). Right?' he asked.

He might as well have thrown a bucket of ice-cold water over me for the shocking chill that went through me at that instant. All I had been thinking about for months before then was the Heart Sutra's *ku* and *mu*! But I had never spoken one word to Soen about any of this. What could have impelled him to want to talk to me about it?

'Do you know what *ku* and *mu* are?' he asked.

In a daze, I shook my head. He held his arms out in front of him.

'If I were carrying a lot of stuff in my arms, could you give me anything?' he asked.

I replied, 'I guess not.'

'No, because they'd be full. But if my arms were empty, there would be no limit to what you could give me, would there? *Ku* and *mu* are just like that.'

With that, the abbot turned around and walked, giggling, back inside the temple.

乃至

Naishi – And the same for the rest

Naishi, translated here as 'And the same for the rest', means 'et cetera'. It allows us to skip the rest of a list, and jump straight to the last item.

The list being shortened here is of the Six Worlds of Perception. In the spirit of Buddhist list-making, the sutra mentions three lists of six items each, all of which have to do with our senses:

Six Sense Organs (eyes, ears and so on, up to the mind)
Six Sensory Bases (what we perceive with the Six Sense
   Organs)
Six Worlds of Perception (the knowledge acquired from
   the Six Sensory Bases)

Naishi comes in handy here so that the sutra doesn't have to mention every one of the items in the final list. When speaking of the Six Worlds of Perception, the sutra jumps from the first (world of sight) straight to the last (world of consciousness). It's saying that all the knowledge we've acquired from our six senses is empty.

Later, *naishi* is used again to abbreviate the list of Twelve Links of Dependent Origination (ignorance through ten steps to old age and death). It's a technique for keeping the sutra short, the fast-forward button. While it's easy to overlook this humble word, *naishi* is basic to the sutra, since being short is the secret to its success. The 100,000-line 'Long *Hannya Haramita* Sutra' is a work of magnificence, but who has the time for all that? The Heart Sutra is just the right length. Any longer, and our minds would wander.

Especially in these days of Twitter and short text messages, our attention spans have dwindled to the point that the great literary and musical achievements of the past – whose defining trait is that they take time – are in danger. In the future, few people will still be listening to full concertos or reading all the way through the endless sentences of Proust – and very few will study or recite the longer sutras.

Only the Heart Sutra will remain.

無意識界

Mu ishiki kai – There is no world of consciousness

As we have seen, Shakyamuni banished the soul right from the beginning. A thousand years later, the Heart Sutra also denied it. But the soul returned, sneaking in through the back door, with the concept of 'Mind Only'.

Xuanzang himself made this possible, because, along with the Heart Sutra, he brought to China the early Indian treatises on 'Mind Only'. According to this school of thought, we apprehend the world through eight levels of consciousness, of which the highest is something called *Alaya*, or 'Storehouse Consciousness'. *Alaya* includes everything we ever thought of (that is, our personal soul).

Alaya – if it endures beyond death – is a problem given the emptiness expounded by the Perfection of Wisdom sutras. There's not supposed to be a truly existent soul, either personal or cosmic. However, in Zen, something along the lines of a soul was needed because otherwise where else could the buddha nature take root? That soul, in turn, was part of a larger flow of the cosmos, the mystic body of the buddha, making each of us already enlightened.

Zen has focused on the *Alaya* of each person's individual mind – the emphasis, as in the *Enchiridion*, is on radical self-reliance. Others go further, seeing *Alaya* as the mind infusing all consciousness, or even as the Cosmic Mind of the universe itself (an approach that had a transformative impact upon certain strands of Tibetan Buddhism).

A poem in the Flower Garland Sutra famously describes 'Mind Only' by using the metaphor of the 'mind-painter'. Just as a painter selects colours and composes them into a painting, the mind collects its thoughts and uses them to make a picture of the external world.

> Mind, just like the painter,
> can paint the different worlds.
> The five *skandha* are born from it;
> there is nothing it does not create.

The mind-painter appealed hugely to later Mahayana Buddhist thinkers. Most crucially, it opens the door to 'mind over matter'. If consciousness comes first, and material things second, then there's room via meditation and rituals to influence the world through the medium of thought. I remember finding the concept of 'Mind Only' incredibly empowering when I first came across it in my studies of Tibetan mysticism.

'Mind Only' infuses modern spiritualism. Gilkey at one point had me reading the teachings of Seth, the spirit guide channelled by medium Jane Roberts. According to Seth, the universe exists as one vast single consciousness who is trying to evolve – that is, as one huge 'mind-painter'. Because of that, Seth says, there's purpose to the universe.

The word for Seth's approach is 'teleological' – based on the idea that things of this world have an intrinsic purpose and direction. Teleological thinkers believe in progress and evolution carrying us to a higher level.

One of the young people who hung around David and Gilkey was Diane Barraclough, an ethereal English girl who had grown up in Kobe. For Diane, everything always boiled down to a love affair. Diane's take on Seth's theories is that God is in love with that lowly thing, matter. It's God's problem, or the universe's problem, to improve and raise the level of matter. For us down here at the level of matter, Diane used to say, 'We must constantly work to keep the universe amused.'

無無明

Mu mumyo – There is no ignorance

Mumyo ('no light') means 'ignorance'. 'No ignorance' comes out as the onomatopoeic *Mu mumyo*. Ignorance is the first item in a Buddhist list, the Twelve Links of Dependent Origination. These are the successive steps we take in our deluded lives, until death comes, and we are reborn into another deluded life. Ignorance, which triggers the whole chain of consequences leading to successive lives, is the original sin of Buddhism, the root of all evil.

Ignorance is when we buy into the illusion of the world. It's ignorance, or as the spiritualists call it 'glamour', that makes us keep stuffing our Five Baskets, even though this is futile. It's ignorance that makes us angry, greedy, lustful, envious, and all the rest of it. Yet the sutra says, 'There is no ignorance.' That's obviously absurd, if we just look at the ignorance all around us, and in our own lives. However, spiritualists would see this from the point of view of the inevitable Advance of the universe. 'There is no ignorance' is not about where we are now, but where we are going. Ignorance will decrease.

Onisaburo of Oomoto taught that the human race is moving from the material to the spiritual. The same idea underlies the *Traiphum* ('Three Worlds') cosmology of Thailand, with its rising tiers of consciousness expanding outwards and upwards from sacred Mount Sumeru, centre of the universe. At the bottom, we are mired in the material world, but after we pass through the magic forest of Himmaphan and begin to climb up Mount Sumeru, we become more and more spiritual, until we disappear at the top into invisible realms beyond material form.

Teleology – the idea that the world is moving forward – plays a key role in modern physics. Time has its unstoppable forward arrow; entropy must always increase, and nothing can reverse that. As time advances, out of the great frothing chaos of the universe 'emergent properties' appear. Subatomic particles are endowed with just a few qualities of mass, spin and charge. They mingle and merge, and from that mix appear entities that we could never have predicted.

First you have protons, electrons and neutrons; join them together and you get atoms with brand new forces and electric fields. Molecules of hydrogen and oxygen gases join together and you have liquid water. Monkeys come down from the trees, run across dry savannahs, and you have human beings. Cells and animals are constantly evolving; in society, consciousness keeps rising.

Gilkey had no nostalgia at all for the past, and insisted that the world was better now than it had been in his boyhood, despite the horrible global wars that happened in the meantime. Even war would disappear, he maintained. His metaphor for that was duelling. According to him, 'Duelling was the standard way to deal with arguments – and then it became unacceptable. How? What happened? Was there a great turning of the tide of public opinion against duellists? I don't know. But I think that eventually war will become an outmoded way of dealing with world problems. Like duelling, it will simply not be thinkable anymore.'

亦無無明盡

Yaku mu mumyo jin – And, likewise, there is no end of ignorance

While *mumyo* is commonly translated as 'ignorance', it really means 'evil'.

Gilkey once said, 'Evil is anything counter to the Advance. It's ancient bungling left lying around. The universe has bungled rather badly, and we are its heirs. One day we are going to be one of the sacred planets, but in the meantime, we are all on the salvage crew.'

The opposite of evil is compassion. The Heart Sutra takes 'wisdom' as its subject, but in Buddhism, wisdom and compassion go together. They are an inseparable pair: *prajna* (*hannya* in Japanese, or 'wisdom') and *upaya* ('skilful means'), Manjusri wielding the flaming sword, Kannon carrying a bottle of tears. Wisdom is understanding your mission as a human being. Compassion is how you put that into action.

A: What's meant by 'compassion'?

G: It's really so simple. Is your heart going to be filled with love for your fellow man, and are you going to do by him as you would be done unto? Or are you going to swing down here on earth because it's your last chance around, and be as thoroughly unspiritual as you can? Sounds awfully dated, doesn't it?'

A: A tad old-fashioned. The Daoists and Buddhists talk about 'paths' and 'ways'.

G: Actually, there are just two paths. There's the high road and there's the low road.

Gilkey and the spiritualists focus on the forward-moving Advance of the cosmic *Alaya* consciousness. The Heart Sutra speaks of the emptiness behind it all. Reconciling these two is a problem, and the Tibetans, among the most enthusiastic believers in *Alaya*, came to recognize this. Enduring cosmic consciousness, according to classical Buddhism, is not supposed to exist. The Tibetans' solution was a two-part system in which consciousness was merely 'interpretable', while emptiness was final and 'definitive'.

This two-part system was just another version of the 'Two Truths'. Behind everything is 'emptiness', but as we have seen, that does not mean nothing exists; in fact, ever-changing chaos exists. Yet out of that chaos, new entities with highly advanced properties emerge.

One of the most far-reaching breakthroughs of the late twentieth century was chaos theory, which shows how sheer randomness generates beautiful and ever-increasing order. Like a lotus pushing upwards through the primal mud, evolution advances until it rises above the water to be crowned with the flower of consciousness. Maybe it's our appreciation of the mysterious, emergent order of things that makes us – and other animals – show an instinct for art.

Onisaburo, co-founder of Oomoto, once said: 'Art is the mother of religion.' It's a peculiar thing to say, because usually it's presented in reverse: religion supposedly is inspiring great art. Onisaburo said, no, art came first.

Emerging order can be seen in the very most basic building blocks of existence. Mysteriously, numbers, all by themselves, with no reference to the 'real world', engender immense and beautiful systems. Add and multiply a few times, and a lush jungle of primes, 'irrational' 'transcendental' and 'complex' numbers springs up. A striking example is the Mandelbrot set. Named after Benoit Mandelbrot, a French/American mathematician who coined the word 'fractal' in 1975 to mean strangely ordered systems that arise out of chaos, it consists of a set of numbers plotted on the two axes of the 'complex plane' (one axis to show the 'real' part of a number and the other the 'imaginary' part).

The Mandelbrot set has entered popular culture with computer simulations that show how it generates fantastical sequences of feathery spirals, frothing waves and curlicues, in infinite levels of detail – all arising from the simplest of rules. These patterns are reflected in the shapes of natural objects, from leaves to swirling galaxies.

The universe's forward march began with $1 + 1 = 2$. The next step was an explosion of weird numbers and unpredictable qualities, the ever-changing 'Emptiness' behind the 'Material World'. And then, out of the chaos itself, slowly but inevitably a new order – the Advance – emerges.

乃至無老死

Naishi mu roshi – And the same for the rest; there is no ageing and death

Once again using the *naishi* 'fast-forward button', the sutra speeds us through another list: the Twelve Links of Dependent Origination. It leaps from ignorance, the first of the Twelve Links (namely ignorance, action, consciousness, the six senses, sense impressions, feelings, desire, attachment, becoming, birth, ageing and death) straight to the end: ageing and death. This is the final destination of our individual emptinesses. Yet the sutra denies even death.

Marguerite Yourcenar began her *Memoirs of Hadrian* by quoting the lines Emperor Hadrian wrote as he was dying in A D 138. Consisting of just nineteen words in the original Latin, it's a super-condensed Heart Sutra in itself:

Animula, vagula, blandula

Dear, restless, little soul,
Guest and partner of my body,
Where will you abide now?
Pale, rigid and bare,
Never to tell me jokes as you used to.

Hadrian saw life as a joke, and death as the regretful punchline. Maybe we could think of Nagarjuna's 'emptiness' as another kind of joke, since 'emptiness' could be just another word for 'absurdity'. Life is the cosmic joke we have been sharing with our dear, restless, little souls.

One way to look at the Heart Sutra is to see it as a work of black humour. One can imagine Hannya Haramita, the goddess of wisdom, dressed in a slinky silk gown as she descends a long spiral staircase. She seats herself at a white piano, and after a sip of dry martini, does a little trill on the keys, and declares, 'There is no ageing and death.' And then gives us a sidelong look to see how we took that.

亦無老死尽

Yaku mu roshi jin – Likewise, there is no end to ageing and death

First the goddess of wisdom denies death, and we can appreciate the dark humour of that. But before we've had a chance to fully take this in, we hear a jazzy rumble of low notes on her divine piano, and she pronounces: 'There is no end to ageing and death.'

David, and Yourcenar, and Gilkey are all dead. As I am now approaching seventy, my mind is turning towards death. Should I travel to places I have always wanted to see? Retire, read and meditate? Plant trees? Finish the Heart Sutra book? And does any of this matter?

The Japanese response to the knowledge that we will all die was the exquisitely refined melancholy of *mono-no-aware*. I was explaining this to Marina Astrologo, a translator I worked with in Italy, and she said, 'Sorry. As a Western intellectual, that passivity just doesn't work for me. I believe in engagement. If you can't engage intensely with everything you do, what's the point of living?'

Of course the Buddhists had thought of that. One of the steps of enlightenment is something called *atappa* (in Japanese *yumo* 勇猛), or 'ardency'. *Atappa* is a by-product of 'mindfulness'. Mindfulness is usually presented as quiet and meditative, but the fact that everything is empty and fleeting can also be

154

a spur to action, to taste to the fullest the nectar of each passing moment.

As the Communists closed in on Beijing after 1945, finally capturing the city in 1949, life in the old capital became increasingly tenuous. Everyone knew that the former way of life was finished. Some could escape to Taiwan or America, but most could not. David Kidd spoke of his Chinese acquaintances – young scholars, friends or lovers of foreigner residents, writers, artists; all were acutely aware of impending doom.

So they danced. They gave parties in dilapidated mansions from which they were soon to be evicted, or in the grounds of old temples, dancing all night long in crumbling courtyards and between red lacquered columns. That's what you do when you know that every minute is precious.

Andrew Marvell's famous sonnet 'To His Coy Mistress' begins, 'Had we but world enough and time', but of course we never do. The sonnet concludes:

> Let us roll all our strength and all
> Our sweetness up into one ball,
> And tear our pleasures with rough strife
> Through the iron gates of life . . .

Hakuin warned against 'being absent' – that is, doing anything without putting your whole heart into it. Marina Astrologo would surely approve of one of Hakuin's roughly brushed calligraphy scrolls, which reads:

> 'Absent for just one moment, you might as well be dead.'

PART 6

No Noble Way and No Merit

無苦・集	There is no Suffering, nor Causes of Suffering,
滅・道。	Nor Cessation of Suffering, nor the Noble Way.
無智、	There is no Wisdom.
亦無得。	Likewise, there's nothing be gained.
以無所得故 . . .	And because there is nothing to be gained . . .

In this sequence, the goddess Hannya Haramita, still seated at her divine piano, delivers a virtuoso performance. She proclaims: 'There is no Suffering, nor Causes of Suffering, nor Cessation of Suffering, nor the Noble Way.' With these four crashing chords, she radically rejects the 'Four Noble Truths'. These are the core of Buddhist philosophy, the one thing that everyone could agree upon.

The Four Noble Truths are not just a list, they are *the* list, the first and most basic teaching of the Buddha. It's the list that came before all the others, taught by every school of Buddhism regardless of sect or country:

Life is Suffering.
The Causes of Suffering are ignorance and attachment.
Rise above these, and you will achieve Cessation of Suffering.
This can be done through the Noble Way of right thoughts and right action.

You could derive all the other principles of Buddhism from these four axioms. When Hannya Haramita refuses to accept these, it would be like Euclid beginning his thesis on geometry by saying, 'There is no point; there is no line; there is no triangle; there is no circle.' Without that, how are you going to get to the hypotenuse of a right angle and *pi*?

Well, relativity, quantum theory, chaos theory and alternative topologies did exactly that. They overturned Euclidean geometry, and the scientific world is still reeling. In the process, completely new approaches to the universe's physical laws are coming into view. In the same way, Hannya Haramita slices off all of Buddhist philosophy at the root with this one sharp swipe of her scythe. From here on we need to start over with fresh axioms to build a new approach.

The goddess does another riff on the keyboard, and adds, 'There is no Wisdom.' With this, she rejects the very essence of Shakyamuni's enlightenment. In contrast to all the others among the world's religious founders, Buddha's unique take was that wisdom would rescue us from suffering. However, according to the goddess, there's no such thing as wisdom. For traditional Buddhists, this line is deeply disturbing.

She's not finished. Almost as an afterthought, a casual comment thrown over her shoulder, she adds: 'There is nothing to be gained.'

Another concept dear to the hearts of Buddhists is 'merit', which one stores up like money in the bank, to achieve a better rebirth in the next round of reincarnation. If there's nothing to be gained, all one's deep understanding, prayers and meditation, not to mention good deeds, count for nothing.

無苦

Mu ku – There is no Suffering

Suffering is the foundation stone on which rests the entire edifice of Buddhist thought, and therefore also the Heart Sutra. Monks used to (and some still do) meditate in graveyards or beside corpses to comprehend the essence of suffering and impermanence.

Of course, there are lists, comprising the Four Major Sufferings and the Four Minor Sufferings. The four major ones are birth, at which the baby starts crying immediately, followed by old age, illness and death. The four minor ones are: parting from loved ones, cohabiting with people you can't stand, failure to get what you want, and physical discomfort such as heat or cold.

Buddhist 'suffering' covers quite a wide range. It could be truly horrible anguish caused by war or illness, for instance, or the loss of a child. Or it might involve merely the irritation of having to put up with unpleasant people or the discomfort of a hot day. Whether the suffering is major or minor, we still need to come up with a way of dealing with it.

A: Why are most religious writings so uninteresting? What are we objecting to when we find we cannot stomach any more speeches about love and brotherhood?

G: I call it 'Sweety Tweety'.

161

A: Sweety Tweety?

G: All is brotherhood and light and joy. Just join our religion and you will become rich, surrounded by supportive friends, blessed by God. That sort of thing. That's 'Sweety Tweety'. It's a desperate attempt to pretend that everything is all right when it isn't. Nothing's going to save you from pain and sorrow. It's an attempt to cover up the awful truth, to sweep it under the carpet.

A: There's also the boredom of that sort of writing.

G: That's because people don't want to read about happiness. They want to read about conflict and suffering. Sweety Tweety flies in the face of most of the rules of story-writing.

A: Is that why Dante and Milton are so much more interesting about hell than they are about heaven?

G: The pleasures of heaven are ineffable. They are beyond us. We can all understand hell because we have been through so much of it already.

集

Shu – [Nor] Causes of Suffering

In classical Buddhism, the causes of suffering lie in desire. The word used for 'causes' in Chinese and Japanese in the sutra is *shu* 集, which means 'collection' or 'concentration'. In Sanskrit the term is *samudaya*, or 'multitude'. There are lots of causes, and they all combine to hurt us.

However, the link between suffering and desire is not so clear cut as we might imagine. It's tempting to think, 'If we could just desire less, our suffering will decrease, and happiness will come our way.' But what about innocent people who suffer terrible tragedies without having desired anything in particular? Or crass Silicon Valley entrepreneurs who make billions from the sheer good fortune of being at the right place at the right time? We are thrown back on the inexplicable mystery of fate, or karma, to use the Buddhist word.

Fazang calls this section of the sutra 'The Pure Gate to Karma'. He says: 'Suffering and its Causes are simply the karma of life. You could say they are the result of living and dying.' With his sharp intuition, Fazang has captured the root of the problem, which is that karma is just life. Sometimes it's the result of our desires; other times it happens regardless.

The usual way to see karma is as 'cause and effect', payback for our ill deeds, along the lines of: 'Do harm to someone, and they will come back in the next life and hurt you.' In any case, they will never leave you alone. Gilkey used to say, 'When you do somebody wrong, you are creating a powerful karmic link. You should ask yourself first, "Do I really want to walk hand in hand down eternity with this jerk?"'

Another interpretation of karma is that the causes and effects play themselves out at a spiritual level. Our soul is like the portrait of Dorian Gray hidden in the attic. Others might never view it, but each vice and evil thought is added to the painting, indelibly marked, until we have become a yellow-fanged demon.

In any case, 'giving up desire' is hopeless. So long as you are still breathing, there will be some desires, and suffering will still come and get you. That said, there is one key to reducing suffering. It can be found in accepting what's right for you, and not asking for more or less. The *Enchiridion* compares life to a banquet:

> Is anything brought round to you? Put out your hand and
> take a moderate share. Does it pass by you? Do not stop it.
> Is it not yet come? Do not yearn in desire toward it, but wait
> till it reaches you. So with regard to children, wife, office,
> riches; and you will some time or other be worthy to feast
> with the gods.

At Ryoanji Temple in Kyoto, famed for its iconic rock garden, there's a stone water basin around the back. The words engraved into it make up a visual pun, consisting of four characters – 吾 ('I'), 唯 ('only'), 足 ('enough'), 知 ('know') – all of which happen to contain within them the character for 'mouth' 口. Placing them together in a circle centred on the 'mouth' 口 that they all share (the water-filled square in the middle of the basin), and reading clockwise from the top, we get 吾唯足知 ('I know only what is enough').

Knowing 'what is enough' is a step in the right direction, but nothing can totally spare you from karma. One day when I was having lunch with Gilkey in the Oomoto cafeteria, I commented: 'I feel like I'm making headway. I've made peace with old enemies. I've put a lot of karma to sleep.' At that moment, I rose to return my tray, and bumped into one of the old ladies of the Oomoto offices, knocking over her tray of food and drink, flinging soup, rice, pickles and tea all over the floor and neighbouring tables. She began shrieking in rage, while people around us looked away in disapproval. Gilkey remarked: 'You see, no sooner have you paid off one debt, then, in an instant, you create a whole mountain of new karma!'

滅

Metsu – [Nor] Cessation of Suffering

Cessation of Suffering is giving up desire. That's how people usually interpret this line. However, there are some things that you are *supposed* to desire.

Gilkey used to say, while drinking the Vienna coffee (which is what they call coffee with cream and whisky in Japan) of which he was inordinately fond: 'It's not that you stop desiring. In fact, the stronger you desire the better. The rules do not say do not desire; the rules say non-attachment. This is what is meant in that most terrible pronouncement in the Bible: "And desire shall fail."'

'That said, you do not kill desire,' he added. 'You detach it from money, sex, feudal lords' palaces – also Vienna coffees – and other evils, and everything that makes life worthwhile. Desire becomes converted to aspiration.'

Without aspiration, equanimity would be just a sort of quiet defeat, despairing acceptance of the world and its miseries. You could say aspiration is the 'Action' that pairs with equanimity's 'Wisdom'.

The later years of David Kidd and William Gilkey hinged on the presence and/or lack of aspiration. When I first knew them, David dwelt in silver-leafed chambers and hobnobbed with the rich and famous. Gilkey, ensconced in his leaky-roofed old house in Kameoka, made tea in a tin cup, and played Brahms on his unreliable upright piano for me, Diane Barraclough and the occasional visitor.

David's meeting with Oomoto in 1976 began gloriously. From the palace in Ashiya he moved to another grand house in Kyoto, where he dreamed of transforming the world. And then it didn't happen. David enjoyed giving advice and he succeeded in dramatically altering the destinies of young people like me and Diane Barraclough. His problem in his later years was that, while he loved helping others, he just couldn't figure out how to do it beyond his immediate circle. Bored with Japan, he went off to Honolulu in 1985 where he died in 1997, and within a few years, the shimmering numinous world of David Kidd completely vanished.

As David's lift descended, Gilkey's rose. A stream of visitors began to arrive at Kameoka, lured by Gilkey's occult studies and his uncannily accurate readings of the *I Ching*. Eventually people were coming from far-flung places to ask Gilkey for his sage but naughty advice.

One of David's favourite sayings was: 'Life is a constant battle against boredom on all fronts. You must create your own inner cinema.' Yet, while David's wit sparkled to the end, somehow boredom got the upper hand.

Back in Kameoka, Gilkey went on cheerfully making tea in his tin cup, playing Brahms on the increasingly undependable piano, and dispensing quirky advice to visitors from all around the world. He was too busy helping people and changing their lives to get bored.

道

Do – Nor the Noble Way

The 'Noble Way' is the pinnacle of the Buddha's teachings – the enlightened life one follows after understanding suffering and its causes. At this point in the sutra nothing should surprise us, but it's still a bit shocking when it tells us we can disregard this too.

Not only the Noble Way, but numerous other important teachings are mentioned in the Heart Sutra, and then denied:

Five Baskets
Six Sense Organs (eyes, ears and so on)
Six Sensory Bases (what we perceive with the Six Sense
    Organs)
Six Worlds of Perception (the knowledge gained from
the Six Sensory Bases)
Twelve Links of Dependent Origination (ignorance
    leading through ten stages to ageing and death)
Four Noble Truths
Mind, the Heart, Wisdom
Emptiness, Merit, Nirvana

In Christianity, they call such a summing up of points of doctrine a 'catechism'. It's a list to help people keep track of what they are supposed to believe in. The most widely used nowadays in English-speaking countries might be the Apostles' Creed, which begins: 'I believe in God, the Father almighty, creator of heaven and earth. I believe in Jesus Christ, his only Son . . .' Buddhists would say for their catechism: 'I take refuge in the Three Gems – the Buddha, the *Dharma* (the teachings), and the *Sangha* (the community).'

In the old times, people in the West took these articles of belief very seriously indeed. The Eastern Orthodox and Roman Catholic Churches argued for centuries and finally split apart over the addition of just one word to the old Nicene Creed. On their part, Buddhists also have not always been tolerant or peaceful, and there have been, and still are, vigorous disagreements between different sects, notably Theravada and Mahayana. That said, Buddhists have laid less emphasis on the bad things that will happen to you if you don't scrupulously follow the catechism.

It goes back to Shakyamuni's parable of the raft. Suppose a man builds a raft to cross from a dangerous place to a safer shore, he said. There would be no point if, after he arrived, he went on carrying the raft in his arms or bearing it on his head. The teachings are for the purpose of crossing over to the other side, and there's no reason to hold on to them once you have got there. Right from the beginning, Buddhists were told to believe in the doctrines only if they were useful to them.

This brings us to the concept of *upaya*, or 'skilful means'. The Tibetans in particular saw wisdom and action (that is, 'skilful means') as the divine combination that made everything possible. Gods and goddesses are often pictured in ecstatic sexual union, symbolizing wisdom expressed through action.

From the perspective of skilful means, you could say, as the sutra does, that there is no Suffering, Causes or Cessation of Suffering or Noble Way. None of these ideas – which are, after all, just religious dogmas – are absolute. As long as you are progressing in your understanding and doing your best to show compassion – the rest doesn't matter.

The Heart Sutra is a classic religious catechism. But instead of saying, 'You had better believe all of this,' the sutra tells us: 'If you're doing the right things, you don't need to believe any of this.'

無智

Mu chi – There is no Wisdom

From the point of view of our personal belief systems, 'There is no Wisdom' means that none of the philosophies we have studied have the final answer, and especially none of the religions. Gilkey saw wisdom as growing with humankind's Advance, until it transcends religions altogether, leading to something larger that we can still only dimly imagine.

G: Ramacharaka speaks of the three spiritual stages of the human race. Stage one is the stage of the child and primitive man, when instinct reigns and the intellect is not fully asserted. In stage two the intellect assumes control. People in this stage are usually quite strenuous in their beliefs, giving rise to all the familiar religious exclusivity and hatreds.

A: What happens when the intellect demands more than religious dogma?

G: That's stage three. Stage three people see good in all forms of religion. They cast off the guilts of outworn moralities, and achieve a consciousness of the Oneness of All.

A: How do you get to stage three? By the time you're ready for it, you don't want to hear anything more on the subject.

G: Actually, between stages two and three there's another stage. Think of all the decent people who will have nothing to do with religion, yet have no vision of what should come next. Either they're lost in the labyrinth of modern physics, or they're feeling guilty because they're not meditating or building hospitals. There they sit, with nowhere to go.

亦無得

Yaku mu toku – Likewise, there's nothing to be gained

'Merit' is a popular concept among those who believe in rein-carnation. The idea is that you store up merit by doing good deeds, and these are credited to your account in the divine ledger. When you die, you cash out, and with a high enough balance you can be reborn at a superior level the next time.

You sometimes see in Zen temples a hanging scroll that reads *Mukotoku* 無功德 ('No Merit'). It's a warning that if you do good things for some hoped-for gain, such as earning merit in heaven, then all the merit is lost.

According to legend, when Bodhidharma, the Indian monk who brought Zen to China in around the early sixth century AD, arrived at the imperial capital in Nanjing, he had an audi-ence with the emperor.

'Since my enthronement, I've built temples, had sutras copied and supported many monks,' the emperor said. 'How much merit have I gained?'

'No merit whatsoever,' replied Bodhidharma.

The emperor was not amused. Bodhidharma had to flee across the Yangzi River to seek a more favourable patron in the north.

Hakuin writes: 'Let go of it! The thief pleads innocence with the stolen goods in his hands.' Hakuin is saying that even if you have actually attained some wisdom, you either don't truly understand it, or most likely don't deserve it. In any case, you shouldn't be claiming it as your own, so let it go.

In contrast to Hakuin's mocking tone, Fazang is more optimistic: 'In the Long Wisdom Sutra, it is written: "For the very reason that there's nothing to be gained, you gain everything."'

以無所得故

I mu shotoku ko – And because there is nothing to be gained . . .

In the early days of the annual Oomoto Seminar in the 1970s, David used to invite Abbot Tachibana Daiki of Daitokuji Zen temple to give us a lecture and write calligraphies for the students. He had been the teacher of Urata, the monk who waved his Heart Sutra fan at David's palace-dismantling party.

One year, at the end of Daiki's lecture, David brought a young Thai student, Ping Amranand, before the abbot and said, 'Would you write something for this young man?' Daiki, wielding a huge brush over a big sheet of paper, scrawled these words: 'Every day is a good day' (*Nichinichi kore kojitsu*「日日是好日」). At the end of the seminar, the calligraphy was given to Ping to keep as a memento. Only a month or so later, Ping's mother was brutally murdered in Bangkok. How could such a shocking and tragic incident possibly have been a 'good day'? Yet Ping kept the calligraphy, and still has it mounted on the wall in his home.

The key to this phrase lies in *upekkha*, the Buddhist virtue of equanimity, which keeps cropping up as we read the Heart Sutra. As we saw earlier, equanimity is written with the kanji 捨 *sha*, meaning 'to throw away'. It represents resignation to life's griefs, and courage in the face of life's atrocities, while still somehow trying to keep up the Buddha's serene smile.

Ping understood that there's profound pathos behind a phrase like 'Every day is a good day'. It's what you say when the sheer wonder or horror of each day is simply beyond words. The twelfth-century Chinese poet Xin Qiji expresses the heart-ache in a poem in which he says that when he was young he used to love to climb to the top of a high tower and loudly recite poems about sorrow and sadness. But now he's older, and he has tasted sorrow to the full. He concludes: 'I try to speak but fall silent. I just say, "The weather is cool, what a lovely autumn."'

PART 7

The Heart is Without Encumbrance

菩提薩埵	The bodhisattvas
依般若波羅蜜多故、	Rely on *Hannya Haramita*, and therefore
心無罣礙。	The heart is without encumbrance,
無罣礙故、	And because it is without encumbrance,
無有恐怖。	There is nothing to fear or worry about.

From here, the sutra starts swimming up from the darkness. We can see the light of enlightenment glimmering above us, its long rays refracted in the water. We have now arrived at the midpoint of the Heart Sutra, where the sutra starts to offer some hope, rather than just denial.

Hasunuma Ryochoku of Nanzenji Temple in Kyoto points out that the Heart Sutra is popular with all sects of Japanese Buddhism except the True Pure Land school.

Followers of True Pure Land believe that if you trust whole-heartedly in Amida, the Buddha of the Western Paradise, he will come to save you. They are interested, Ryochoku says, not so much in *ku* 空 ('emptiness'), as in *gan* 願 ('wish') – that is, the wish to be saved.

Who needs *ku*? *Gan* is everyone's true desire. In this section of the Heart Sutra finally there's a bit of *gan*. In spite of the emptiness, there is something we can wish for. The sutra, which so far has been entirely negative, is telling us that there's a way out from fear and worry. You might say this is the point where the goddess Hannya Haramita finally smiles.

菩提薩埵

Bodaisatta – The bodhisattvas

A bodhisattva, enlightened, all-compassionate, risen way above the rat race, feels very distant and unattainable. Yet, it's said that one bodhisattva is very close by; she resides within each of us. This is *bodhicitta* – the 'buddha heart' – the desire to be wise and good.

The Dalai Lama says: 'There is no more virtuous mind than *bodhicitta*. There is no more powerful mind than *bodhicitta*, there is no more joyous mind than *bodhicitta* . . . Every ordinary and supra-mundane power can be attained through *bodhicitta*. Thus it is absolutely precious.'

In case we don't feel *bodhicitta* all on our own, the cosmos has ways of pushing us in that direction. In Buddhist writings we hear a lot about how wonderful it is to be a bodhisattva, but very little about how to get there. Gilkey had lots of practical advice to offer on the subject, beginning with the concepts of 'Arctic hysteria' and 'the Stripping'.

He pointed out that psychics typically undergo a period of sickness and troubles before they acquire their powers. A notorious example may be seen in the female shamans of the Inuit people in Greenland in the nineteenth century, who suffered from a strange illness involving seizures, nausea and amnesia. Western explorers called this 'Arctic hysteria'. After several months or even years of Arctic hysteria, the woman would wake up one day with paranormal powers of healing and clairvoyance.

For the rest of us, the push to spirituality can come in the form of 'the Stripping'.

G: Before you embark on your new course, they literally strip you for action. Your possessions, your friends, your ideals, dreams, everything falls away. The best thing to do is to open your hand and let them all go.

A: Is the main point of the Stripping to teach you how to let go?

G: Most saints were drawn into it kicking and screaming like the rest of us. They didn't take their vows until they had to.

依般若波羅蜜多故

E Hannya Haramita ko – Rely on Hannya Haramita, and therefore

David Kidd was much attached to electrical wizardry. In the *tokonoma* alcove used for displaying important artworks, a majestic Kamakura Buddha sat on a large slab of precious *keyaki* wood, and at the touch of a button, the slab with the Buddha on it would rise, and from underneath would appear a large TV. The curtains to the garden also opened by remote control, and sometimes it came as a surprise, after a long night of sitting in the living room and admiring art works, when the curtains would suddenly part to reveal morning sunlight sparkling on the grass outside.

David said he once had a dream in which he pressed the button to show some guests the morning-garden trick, but when the curtains slid open, it was pitch dark outside. Beyond the glass doors stretched the fathomless expanse of the universe, gleaming with stars. They were adrift in the void.

That's the terrifying, but exhilarating feeling of the Heart Sutra. You're out there floating in the great night sky, just you and the cosmos, gazing at the wonder of it all.

The words 'Rely on *Hannya Haramita*', therefore, don't quite fit in, as what in the world are you supposed to rely on? Hakuin noticed this, and reacting with typical scorn, he wrote, '*Aak, aak!* I'm choking. If you see one principle to rely on, immediately spit it out!' In Hakuin's view, *Hannya Haram-ita* is perfect wisdom beyond all material forms and surpassing all expression in words. At the point when we achieve that wisdom, we don't need to rely on anything, except ourselves, and therefore the words 'rely on' are superfluous. Hakuin concluded: 'It is really a shame, when drawing a snake, to add a pair of legs.'

心

Shin – The heart

When Dogen, founder of Japanese Soto Zen, returned from China in the thirteenth century, he was asked what sutras he had brought back with him. In contrast to Xuanzang, who had returned from his journey west with hundreds of sutras loaded on to a great line of horses, Dogen answered, 'I have come back empty-handed, without even a single shred of Buddhist knowledge.'

They asked him, 'So what did you learn?'

Dogen replied, 'I did learn just a little flexibility of heart.'

'Flexibility of heart' is the big lesson that Japanese foreign-exchange students have learned from going abroad, from Dogen in the thirteenth century right up to tech entrepreneur Masayoshi Son in the twentieth.

Flexibility is actually equanimity again, in a new guise – resilience and good cheer in the face of the fact that we are not in control. Presidents we don't like get elected, planes crash, the very cells of our body are deciding whether to be benign or cancerous, and there's nothing we can do about it.

The *Enchiridion* teaches the technique of equanimity in this way:

Practice then from the start to say to every harsh
impression, 'You are an impression, and not at all the thing

you appear to be.' Then examine it and test it by this: whether the impression has to do with the things that are up to us, or those that are not; and if it has to do with the things that are not up to us, be ready to reply, 'It is nothing to me.'

As the Heart Sutra hammers home again and again, we're all of us captives in a universe of ephemeral objects and events. We have no real control over anything, except our own heart – and even that has its limits. Of practically everything in our lives, we should be ready to say, 'It is nothing to me.'

This book began with the day that David Kidd's palace in Ashiya was destroyed. But David had previously lost another, much grander palace, when the Communists forced him and his Chinese family out of their hundred-room mansion in Beijing in 1950. In his *New Yorker* stories about those years, David recalled how, just before he left Beijing to return to the United States, he paid a visit to the old matriarch of the family, Aunt Chin, who was now living in a hovel. He asked about the gold hidden in the wall which was supposed to save them, but which she seemed to have left behind.

'*I* didn't give up the gold,' she said. 'The wall did. I only let things go their own way. Houses and people and tables and chairs move and change of themselves, following destinies that cannot be altered. When things change into other things or lose themselves or destroy themselves, there is nothing we can do but let them go.'

無罣礙

Mu kege – Is without encumbrance

Encumbrance is the dust that gathers on the mirror of the heart. It's the result of *bonno* 煩悩, or 'distracting thoughts' – beauty, fear, envy, charm, wealth, and so many other entanglements that get us caught up in the 'glamour' of this illusory world.

When the fourth-century Daoist sages met for their transcendental chats in the bamboo grove, they held long whisks in their hands to brush away the summer flies. In time these whisks, called *hossu* 払子, came to symbolize 'brushing away the flies of care'. People used them as the symbol of a 'pure conversation', namely talk that's free from any mention of money, sex, politics or other lowly things of this world.

The Daoist fly whisks got into Zen Buddhism, where you sometimes see images of Bodhidharma or Zen masters holding a whisk in their hands. I keep a few *hossu* whisks strategically placed around my house. They have had only a limited effect in raising the tone of the conversation, but every once in a while, I catch sight of one of these whisks, and it reminds me of what we ought to have been talking about.

Anyone who has done meditation knows how hard it is to free the mind of encumbrances and distractions, even if they might amount to no more than one buzzing fly. For most of us, it is a nearly superhuman feat to get through a single day without thinking about the cares of this world. When we do manage to rise above our worries and attachments, that's what the sutra calls 'the heart without encumbrance'. We are lucky – we find real joy – if that sense of peace and freedom lasts for more than an instant.

I used to have a scroll with a painting of a *hossu* whisk, on which a Zen abbot had written: 'In the shade of the bamboo, I brushed everything away – but the dust won't move!'

無罣礙故

Mu kege ko – And because it is without encumbrance

Hasunuma Ryochoku says that a hint of the way out of our messy existence lies in *ke* 罣, the first character of the compound *kege* 罣礙 or 'encumbrance'.

Ke 罣, which means 'obstruction', consists of two parts, 四 ('four') on the top and 圭 ('sceptre') on the bottom. From its form 圭, which looks like criss-cross lines on a graph, Ryochoku takes the lower part to mean 'all paths – north, south, east and west'. The character 'four' squatting heavily on top means that all four ways are blocked. There's only one place to go, says Ryochoku: 'Rise above it all.'

'Above it all' was Gilkey's favourite direction.

G: I was going to sleep, and I found myself at a great convocation: Plato, Socrates and Pericles were there. They were all standing in a beautiful grove, and I was thinking, 'Oh, how marvellous it would be to join this group!' But as I approached, Socrates shook his head, and said, 'No, no.' Then Socrates pointed up.

And now it's perfectly evident to me: It's not among the brains and the social finest that I am supposed to function. I was being pointed away from the wisdom of this earth to the Flow. Later, I told David this, and David thought it was most amusing.

A: The idea that one is not supposed to mingle with the social finest must have seemed hilarious to him.

G: Occasionally when I do something that's rather too much of this world, David still points upwards!

無有恐怖

Mu u kufu – There is nothing to fear or worry about

Alexandra Munroe was one of the young people who hung around David along with me and Diane Barraclough. She at one point considered taking Buddhist orders under the guidance of Abbot Tachibana Daiki. 'But,' says Alexandra, 'when I realized I would end up entering a nunnery, that stopped me. I went to explain to Daiki that I would decline this enormous honour. He harrumphed, reached into his closet, pulled out a scroll and said, "Here you go, take this." The scroll said, "Faith, Doubt and Courage."'

Of Daiki's three principles, he could have saved on calligraphy ink by not writing 'Faith'. In the Heart Sutra, there is no faith, only doubt and courage. Having only doubts, and nothing in particular to hope for, but not giving up – what could be a better definition of the word 'courage'?

Courage, in fact, might be the ultimate teaching of the Heart Sutra. It's closely related to *atappa* ('ardency' or 'engagement'), mentioned earlier. In fact, the Chinese word for *atappa* is a combination of two characters that mean 'courage' 勇 and 'intensity' 猛. The Heart Sutra helps you to conjure up the bravery you need to face hard things, even when there's no consolation to be found, and the courage to be a good person, even when there's no logical reason for doing so.

Recently, as I was thinking about the Heart Sutra and courage, my attention was caught by a clip that someone uploaded to Facebook of a child, who appeared to be about four years old, trying to climb the steps to a slide. The boy had no arms or legs. His mother kept encouraging him, and somehow, after many a mishap, he managed to clamber to the top, and rode down the slide with an angelic smile on his face.

It made me think of the other side of fear and suffering, which is ardency, with its companion virtue, good cheer. Epictetus in the *Enchiridion* says that there are two ways to handle misfortune: the easy or the hard way. The hard way is to get angry and upset. The easier way to bear with bad things is simply to maintain one's good cheer. Bad things are going to happen anyway, so one might as well face them optimistically.

The Dalai Lama is an exemplar of this kind of courage. He keeps up an undying cheerfulness and optimism, despite the fact that the situation in Tibet gives nothing to be cheerful about. Yet the Dalai Lama goes on smiling.

PART 8

Attain Supreme,
Perfect Enlightenment

遠離一切顛倒夢想、	They escape all absurdities and fantasies,
究竟涅槃。	Reaching ultimate nirvana.
三世諸仏	The buddhas of the Three Worlds
依般若波羅蜜多故、	Rely on *Hannya Haramita*, and therefore
得阿耨多羅、三藐三菩提。	They attain supreme, perfect enlightenment.

Writers on the Heart Sutra have divided it into a number of chapters – five, seven or ten. Whichever way they slice it, they all agree on one big dividing point, and that's between the early part, which can be understood by the mind, and the latter part, which cannot.

This section marks the end of the first part. The pyramid of reasoned thought that began in the first lines with Kannon declaring that 'the Five Baskets are all empty' reaches its pinnacle here with nirvana and enlightenment.

The eighth-century Indian monk Kamalashila described the Heart Sutra as a series of learnings or 'paths', culminating in this section, which he called the 'Path of No More Learning'. This idea was absorbed into Tibetan Buddhism, and the Dalai Lama uses the same words today.

Kamalashila is also known for taking part in the Council of Lhasa, a two-year debate in 792–4 sponsored by the Emperor of Tibet. At issue was 'gradualism' versus 'immediacy'. Gradualism, favoured in India, held that one reaches enlightenment through long study and mystical practice. Immediacy, as propounded by Chinese Zen, held that one could achieve enlightenment suddenly, without relying on any particular technique.

At the Council, on one side was Moheyan, a Chinese Zen adherent. On the other side was Kamalashila, who argued against minimalist Zen in favour of the mystical teachings of India. Kamalashila was declared the winner, Moheyan fled the country, and as a result Zen never conquered Tibet as it later did Korea and Japan.

In this section, we have reached our destination. Enlightenment is here, with us now. Kamalashila called this section the 'Path of No More Learning' because we're approaching the limits of rational thought. Following this section, we leave behind the rational for the mystical.

遠離一切顛倒夢想

Onri issai tendo muso – They escape all absurdities and fantasies

As I was writing this book, I had a dream in which I had lost my keys. I had mislaid them somewhere in one of the paragraphs of the Heart Sutra. I searched frantically, but couldn't find them, until at last I woke up in a sweat. I'm still wondering which paragraph of the sutra I had lost them in.

I think the keys I was looking for were to my own equanimity. Despite all the wisdom of the Heart Sutra, the virtue of *upekkha* eludes me, especially when it comes to politics, about which I find my feelings are only growing more and more heated. Thich Nhat Hanh says that *upekkha* goes hand in hand with the 'wisdom of equality' or 'the ability to see everyone as equal, not discriminating between ourselves and others. In a conflict, even though we are deeply concerned, we remain impartial, able to love and to understand both sides.'

With a sinking feeling I realize that, for all my decades of pondering the Heart Sutra, I'm further than ever from 'escaping absurdities and fantasies'. I recall Thoreau's comment about the uselessness of older people: 'One may almost doubt if the wisest man has learned anything of absolute value by living.' Maybe – someone should finally say it – the even-handed approach of the Heart Sutra is simply impossible for most human beings.

Actually, I'm not the first to have this thought. Honen and Shinran, the twelfth/thirteenth-century Japanese monks whose teachings underlie the sects of Pure Land and True Pure Land Buddhism, believed that we are living in a corrupt latter era, called the 'End of the *Dharma*' (*mappo* 末法), in which Buddha's words are forgotten, as people are too dull to understand them. Shinran wrote: 'Ignorance and worldly cares are imbued deep within us; there's much greed, anger, bad temper, jealousy, many envious emotions, and they are with us every instant in our every thought, never disappearing, unending.'

If that's so, there's no point in reciting or reading the Heart Sutra. Honen, Shinran's master, ridiculed the idea that we are going to get something out of studying Buddhist texts: 'In this age of the End of the *Dharma*, among the billions of human beings, when it comes to embarking on Practice and attempting the Way – there's never been a single person who achieved any of it!' Honen and Shinran's answer was to give up on the sutras, and instead devotedly pray to Amida Buddha in his Western Paradise.

Unfortunately for me, I am not disposed to rely on any god for salvation, so I haven't yet turned to Amida. I continue to seek the answer in the Heart Sutra, even though, as Shinran and Honen would point out, it doesn't feel as if it offers much help in bad times. Somehow, I'm hoping to reach a balance in order to be a decent human being. Meanwhile, the keys are still lost somewhere inside the Heart Sutra. I hope I wake up soon.

究竟涅槃

Kugyo nehan – Reaching
ultimate nirvana

Samsara ('the sea of the world') and nirvana co-exist on a sliding scale. At the lower end of the scale is the turbulence of *samsara*; at the higher end, the peace of nirvana. You don't suddenly leap from one to the other. There are steps along the way.

Across East Asia there's the belief in a hierarchy of worlds centred on the cosmic Mount Sumeru. The most perfect expression of this was the *Traiphum*, the 'Three Worlds' cosmology, compiled in Thailand in the fourteenth century. According to the *Traiphum*, the World of Sensuality sits at the bottom, and the World of Form (expressed as *shiki* 色 in the Heart Sutra) in the middle. That's the world we live in. At the heart of our world rises the cosmic mountain, Mount Sumeru, soaring into the third world, the World Beyond Form.

Encircling Sumeru are four oceans and four continents, and seven rings of mountains. Situated in the foothills, between our world and the slopes of Mount Sumeru, is a magic forest called Himmaphan, a twilight zone where wild holy men roam, and humans mate with birds, animals and plants, creating all sorts of weird and lovely hybrids. The Thais have always adored Himmaphan and devoted much of their art to it. The Japanese and Chinese have tended to focus more on the mountain itself. Although, come to think of it, the sand gardens of

Zen temples could be seen as a special version of Himmaphan for minimalists. A garden of delights without the delights.

Once past the Himmaphan forest, Mount Sumeru rises into the World Beyond Form. As in an exclusive high-rise condominium, lesser gods live on the lower levels, while more ethereal gods have apartments on the higher floors. Above and beyond the peak of Mount Sumeru stretch the Immaterial Realms, invisible spheres spreading outwards like canopies of expanding umbrellas. This is where the highest and most perfected spiritual beings are found. Each sphere is increasingly empty and pure, until finally everything disappears into nirvana.

Mount Sumeru is reflected in the design of Buddhist temples across Asia, from the massive monuments of Angkor Wat and Borobudur in South East Asia, to temple complexes in Japan. In a Japanese pagoda, the base is our World of Forms. Above this, the roof at each level represents a stage of enlightenment further removed from the physical plane. The eaves and rafters of the highest roof symbolize the realms where the loftiest gods and bodhisattvas dwell. But even they are not supreme.

From the pinnacle of the highest roof rises a tall thin spire surrounded by golden rings. These represent the invisible 'expanding umbrella' realms. Finally, the spire narrows to a point, and where it tapers off, in the empty air just beyond the tip, is nirvana.

三世諸仏

Sanze shobutsu – The buddhas of the Three Worlds

The 'Three Worlds' are usually seen to be the past, present and future, which would mean that there's a time element to the Heart Sutra after all. In any case, the keys to this phrase are the buddhas. The door to the dusty old temple slides open, and we stand in silence with row upon row of buddha statues gleaming in the darkness. They're the buddhas who came before and will come after us.

Buddhas are supposed to be perfected beings, but one wonders if such a thing has ever existed. *Bodhicitta*, 'buddha heart', is the aim and desire for perfection, not a measure of to what extent you've achieved it. In my mind, those statues represent men and women of good intention who strove to be better people in the midst of chaos and heartbreak, just as we try to do now.

This is the point in the sutra where I think of friends and mentors now gone; monks and poets who showed the way; and young people who will be seeking far in the future. They are the buddhas of the Three Worlds. We've entered the temple, and found ourselves surrounded by friends.

依般若波羅蜜多故

E Hannya Haramita ko – Rely on Hannya Haramita, and therefore

In early Buddhism, nirvana was simply extinction. The Buddha vanished into nirvana and nothing remained. But after Nagarjuna in the second/third century, the feeling has been that nirvana takes place within the realities of the physical world, as illusionistic and evanescent as it is. The enlightened person sees through it all, and then comes back to help others.

A set of short poems with accompanying drawings originating in twelfth-century China called the Ten Bull Pictures (*Jugyuzu* 十牛図) describes the stages on the pathway to enlightenment. The first five pictures are:

1. *Seek the Bull*
2. *Find the Footprints*
3. *See the Bull*
4. *Catch the Bull*
5. *Tame the Bull*

The sequence leading to the capturing of the bull is quite strenuous, especially *Tame the Bull*, which is where most of us get stuck. These are the five steps of *gyo* ('practice'), the hard work of self-improvement.

6. *Ride Home on the Bull*

When the bull is tamed and you 'ride home on the bull', you've achieved freedom. I have a scroll of this at home, depicting a boy sitting on the back of a bull and playing a flute. He's facing nonchalantly backwards without a care in the world. I like to bring it out on gloomy days.

The next two pictures are:

7. *Forget the Bull and Reside in Yourself*
8. *Bull and Oneself are Both Forgotten*

The image of *Bull and Oneself are Both Forgotten* is often rendered as an empty circle. We have reached the emptiness at the core of the Heart Sutra.

But the Ten Bull Pictures don't stop there. There are two more images yet to come.

9. *Return to the Origin*

Return to the Origin is illustrated by a scene of streams, mountains, birds and flowers.

10. *With Free Hands, Enter the Market Place*

The last image shows a plump jovial-looking sage, not unlike Gilkey, entering the market place. Now enlightened, he's returning to society.

得阿耨羅多、三藐三菩提

Toku anokutara, sanmyaku sanbodai –
They attain supreme, perfect
enlightenment

This line, which concludes the 'rational' part of the sutra, is one of its more baffling phrases, since the words *anokutara sanmyaku sambodai* are meaningless to most modern readers. They have been transliterated phonetically from the Sanskrit *anuttara samyak sambodhi*. *Anuttara* means 'supreme'; *samyak* is 'perfect'; and *sambodhi* means 'enlightenment'. It's an old phrase, dating back to the earliest days of Buddhism, referring to Shakyamuni's original enlightenment.

'Supreme perfect enlightenment' marks the pinnacle of the Heart Sutra. It describes the clear unclouded mind that sees and takes joy in the Perfect Wisdom of *Hannya Haramita*, that is, in the world with all its strangeness. Returning full circle to the liberation of the spirit promised at the beginning by Kannon, we emerge blissful and free into the light.

If only that could be so! Maybe enlightenment is not something that we could ever actually attain, but something to just dream of and wish for. The tenth-century Chinese Zen patriarch Fayan used to call enlightenment 'the moon' and our struggles to improve ourselves 'the finger pointing to the moon' (指月).

One of my treasured hanging scrolls is a calligraphy by an Edo-period abbot of Daitokuji, with the words: 'I gaze at the beautiful one in a corner of the sky' 「望美人兮天一方」. It's a line from Su Dongpo's *Red Cliff Ode*. The 'beautiful one' is the moon, and it represents the impossible, unreachable ideal that we seek but can never touch. Tamasaburo, when asked why he wanted to become a kabuki actor, answered: 'I was in love with a world beyond reach.' He was expressing the aching yearning for something greater and more beautiful than we could ever be.

In Zen they speak of *satori*, which is a sudden flash of understanding. The point of meditating on impossible koans is to force people into *satori*. It's a moment when people see and understand their inner souls and the cosmos, like the sleepless man in David Kidd's unpublished story who, while walking down the stairs, becomes briefly transformed into the Divine Shiva. Of course, the bliss of insight wears off, your foot touches the landing, and the *satori* reverts to the everyday.

Gilkey said *satori* was like when God took Moses to a cliff from which he could contemplate the Promised Land in the distance. Moses could see it but he died before he could ever set foot in it. '*Satori* is a sneak preview,' said Gilkey. 'You still have to play your part.'

While the sutra proclaims, 'They attain supreme, perfect enlightenment', I suspect that the 'attain' part is actually far beyond most of us, and even were it to come, it would be fleeting. That's the insight expressed by Fayan and the Daitokuji abbot who penned the calligraphy. As for myself, I think of it whenever I see the full moon in a corner of the sky. It's the symbol of what we aim for, but can never have.

One needn't be sad. *Hannya Haramita* is all about emptiness, clear as a fresh spring day. It brings with it a certain lightness of spirit. Dogen, in his essay on the Heart Sutra, wraps it up with a cheerful poem he learned from his master in China:

> My whole being is like the mouth of a bell hanging in air:
> It does not ask whether the wind blows east or west, north
>   or south.
> Equally to all, it clangs Wisdom for others' sake:
> '*Chin Ten Ton*,' says the bell, '*Chin Ten Ton*.'

PART 9

The Mantra of Great Mystery

故知、 般若波羅蜜多	Thus they know that *Hannya Haramita*
是大神呪、	Is the mantra of great mystery.
是大明呪、	It is the mantra of great light.
是無上呪、	It is the mantra of which none is higher.
是無等等呪。	It is the mantra ranked beyond all ranks.
能除一切苦、	With it one escapes all suffering.
真実不虚。	It is truth and reality, without falsehood.

One of the visitors in David Kidd's Ashiya palace was Domo Geshe Rinpoche, a Tibetan lama from Sikkim. Domo Geshe was a 'reincarnate lama', whose lineage, I later discovered, could be traced all the way back to Shariputra, to whom the Heart Sutra was first addressed. He had been jailed by the Chinese in the 1950s, endured torture and was finally released at the personal request of Prime Minister Nehru of India. When Domo Geshe found out that I was studying Tibetan, he said, 'You will need this,' and handed me a piece of paper.

On it was written a hundred-syllable incantation called the *Yiggya*, among the most powerful of all Tibetan chants, and he advised me to recite it every day. I kept chanting the *Yiggya* for years, and even now keep a copy near me. I can still recite some sections of it from memory, and I am especially fond of the five mystical syllables near the end which go: *Ha Ha Ha Ha Ho!*

The *Yiggya* was my first mantra. The hundred syllables can be interpreted to mean something, but the true sense is mostly a mystery. This is because mantras belong to what is known in Sanskrit as *samdhya-bhasa*, or 'twilight language'. A form of coded communication, it has the power to quell evil and conjure good, but the deep source of that power is beyond the understanding of most people. Right at the beginning, the first translator of the Heart Sutra, Xuanzang, wrote concerning the mantra in the Heart Sutra: 'Mantras are the first of the five kinds of words not to be translated. Surely this mantra consists of the secret words of the Buddhas. It is not something that inferior, unenlightened people can know.'

People nowadays tend to downplay the element of mantra because they're not sure what to make of it. However, in the old days it was considered to be the main point. Xuanzang, Fazang, Kukai and many others have seen the mantra as the part of the sutra that really matters. It's believed that the mantra compresses the whole of the sutra into a few short words – and not only the Heart Sutra itself, but *all* wisdom. In the words of the eighteenth/nineteenth-century Tibetan monk Gung-thang: 'The quintessence of the 84,000 collections of doctrine is the Perfection of Wisdom sutras, and the quintessence of the

Large Perfection of Wisdom sutra and the others is the Heart Sutra, and the concentrated meaning of that is in this mantra.'

Above and beyond the compressed wisdom, the mantra is in fact a magic spell. Writers today appear to show a certain embarrassment about this element of superstition. They gloss over the magical side, interpreting it as 'symbolism'. Domo Geshe certainly didn't see it that way. He used the mantra for the reason that it works. He told me: 'Usually I feel I can just rely on my own good karma. But when I'm seated in an aeroplane, it's a different story. My fate is then bound up with hundreds of other passengers. Sometimes I can feel their bad karma swirling around the plane, and I sense that it could overwhelm mine. So I recite the *Yiggya* for us all to be safe.'

From here on we step into the world of magic and mystery. For people in the pre-modern era, this was where the deep power of the sutra lay. For readers nowadays, it's quite a stretch, but it has its forbidden appeal in our scientific age.

We are like the train passengers in Proust's *In Search of Lost Time* who deeply disapproved of the flamboyant Baron de Charlus with his outrageous airs and graces. But 'if M. de Charlus did not appear, they were almost disappointed to be travelling only with people who were just like everybody else, and not to have with them this painted, paunchy, tightly-buttoned personage, reminiscent of a box of exotic and dubious origin exhaling a curious odour of fruits the mere thought of tasting which would turn the stomach.'

Without the mantra, we would be travelling with people 'just like everybody else'; there would be no exotic box emitting curious, even dread-inducing, odours. The sutra would remain just another work of philosophy, and never make the leap into the fantastic.

故知、般若波羅蜜多

Ko chi Hannya Haramita – Thus they know that Hannya Haramita

At one point in his travels in Western China around AD 630, Xuanzang was crossing a trackless desert. Although there was nary a bird, animal or tree to be seen, he found himself surrounded by demons. He prayed to his guardian, Bodhisattva Kannon, but to no avail. However, when he recited the Heart Sutra, the demons disappeared with a shriek. 'In my moment of danger, what saved me was that I relied on this treasure,' he later wrote.

Ever since then, the Heart Sutra, and especially the mantra, has been seen to have supernatural powers. By the mid eighth century, its fame had reached Japan to the extent that Emperor Junnin in Nara issued the following decree:

> It is said, 'If you recite the Four Lines [i.e. the mantra], you will achieve what you wish without worry.' Because of this, if the Emperor chants the sutra, wars and disasters will not enter the kingdom. If the common people chant it, disease and epidemics will not arise. To cut off evil and attain good auspices, there can be nothing superior. Proclaim this to the nation, and let men and women, no matter whether old and young, when rising, sitting, standing, or walking, all recite the Great Sutra of *Hannya Haramita*.

The mantra brings us to the point where we have to discuss the power of mind over matter. Nagarjuna had famously said: 'All is possible when emptiness is possible. If there were no emptiness, nothing would be possible.' In saying 'all is possible', Nagarjuna is describing what nowadays we would call 'God of the gaps'. The gaps are the fuzzy areas in physics and mathematics where determinism breaks down, and unknowability and randomness set in.

In the case of subatomic particles, the Heisenberg uncertainty principle tells us that we can never know exactly a particle's position and its momentum. Quantum theory holds that literally anything is possible; it's just a matter of probability wave functions if an event happens or not. In mathematics, we still cannot predict the appearance of new prime numbers or the next digit of *pi*.

As for the colourful Mandelbrot set, with each iteration it reveals shifting phantasmagoric designs that we never could have imagined. Mandelbrot called these fractal images 'the uncontrolled element in life'. Everywhere – built right into the basic structure of the universe – is instability, randomness and surprise. These are the 'gaps' in which it seems that mind might be able to influence matter.

One of the disturbing aspects of quantum theory has been the fact that particles remain in a vague, blurry state of many possibilities – until observed. At that instant those possibilities 'collapse' into one thing or another. Schrödinger's cat is either alive or dead – or, to speak in tetralemmas, neither alive nor dead – until we look into the box and see.

Since each particle in the universe, and the cat, are quantum-linked to all the other particles, that means that they are all somehow affected by what the observer sees. This has led some theoretical physicists to speculate that our physical universe itself only exists because we are conscious and can observe it. That is, we are all 'mind-painters'.

是大神呪

Ze dai jinshu – Is a mantra of great mystery

Sanskrit has two words for mantra: mantra and *dharani*. Mantra stresses sound while *dharani* implies meaning – but the two terms are used almost interchangeably.

The idea behind mantras is that the universe is pervaded with pure sound; mantras and *dharanis* reflect cosmic principles such as the inward and outward movement of breath. Indian philosophers equated the sound with the goddess Shakti, goddess of cosmic energy, in mystical union with Shiva.

The most basic mantra is *Om*. It often appears at the beginning of longer mantras, thus enveloping one mantra within another, as in some Indian and Tibetan versions of the Heart Sutra, where the final mantra itself begins with *Om*.

One of the simplest mantras, written in Sanskrit, is *Hamsa sa Ham* ('I am that divine Hamsa bird'). If you take the four syllables – *Ham–sa–sa–Ham* – and place them back to front, you get *Hamsa sa Ham* again, thus making a palindrome. Myriads of other mantras and *dharanis* exist, some far longer than the hundred-syllable *Yiggya*. In fact, one can be found in almost every Mahayana sutra. It is said that there are seventy million mantras.

This mantra from the Lankavatara Sutra, which is closely related to the Heart Sutra, gives something of the rhythmical flair of a grand mantra:

Tutte tutte vutte vutte patte patte katte katte amale amale vimale vimale nime nime hime hime vame vame kale kale kale kale atte matte vatte tutte jnette sputte katte katte latte patte dime dime cale cale pace pace badhe bandhe ance mance dutare dutare patare patare arkke arkke sarkke sarkke cakre cakre dime dime hime hime tu tu tu tu du du du du ru ru ru ru phu phu phu phu svaha.

Enigmatic though it appears, mantras like this are thought to store immeasurable wisdom.

Kukai sums up the mystique of mantras and *dharanis* as follows: 'Within a single sound all virtues are stored. Therefore, *dharanis* are called the inexhaustible treasury.'

是大明呪

Ze dai myoshu – It is the mantra of great light

According to Kazuaki Tanahashi in his book on the Heart Sutra, 'great light' is a Chinese translation of the Sanskrit word *vidya*, which means knowledge, philosophy, science.

Rendering the word for 'knowledge' as 'great light' was another brilliant stroke on the part of the early translators, as it brings the focus back to light. It's symbolized by the image of the Buddha, his body emitting beams that illuminate the cave in which he is meditating, or the single white hair between his eyebrows which shines a ray of light on eighteen thousand worlds. The sixteenth-century Chinese monk Hanshan Deqing, in his essay *A Straight Talk on the Heart Sutra*, wrote about this line: 'With a moment's reflection, all barriers of emotion in life and death will be shattered, as the light of a lamp illumines a room where darkness existed for a thousand years.'

For Gilkey, 'light' was not just a metaphor for wisdom, but an actual energy that could change the world. This energy resides within mantras, and it's what spiritualist mystics, and also certain Tibetans, aim to activate when they do their meditations.

A: I wonder how many people in the world are actually doing this actively? I suppose there are some Tibetan monks.

G: With no other wills to contend with, the powers of re-creation are almost irresistible. At this stage, the potential at one's disposal is breathtaking. What do you want to change – the lives of your friends, the destiny of Oomoto, New York City?

A: I'm not sure I'm ready to take on New York City.

是無上呪

Ze mujoshu – It is the mantra of which none is higher

What if, during a deeply focused meditation, one observed something different from usual in the things around us? After one had 'visualized' that mental image, would the universe later respond to our 'mind-painting'? Some of the Tibetans thought it would, and mystical meditation, at least as those Tibetans saw it, is a serious business, 'mind over matter'. Actually, much of Tibetan practice is internal, aimed at awakening one's *bodhicitta*. But there has also been a group of Tibetan practitioners whose focus is on intense visualization of deities and spiritual powers in order to make things happen.

This brings up the great divide in spirituality: between passive and active meditation. 'Passive' is where you seek oneness with the universe. 'Active' is where you use your mind to change the world. When Kamalashila bested Moheyan, the Zen minimalist, at the Council of Lhasa in 794, he set Tibet forever on the path of 'gradualism', rather than sudden Zen-style enlightenment. For Tibetan monks, gradualism meant years or decades of study and mystical practice, and over the centuries this led them to invent a rich repertory of mental techniques. One branch of these extended into the occult – of mind over matter.

On this subject, I learned much from another Tibetan lama who frequented David Kidd's house, Kalsang Rinpoche. He tutored me in Tibetan for a while before he moved on from Japan to America. I remember him telling me: 'Those Zen people who spend hours and hours facing the wall and emptying their minds, how dull! Now we who use our mental energies to create visualizations, we are really doing something.'

是無等等呪

Ze mutodoshu – It is the mantra ranked beyond all ranks

Not everyone is enamoured with mantras. Way back in the fourth/fifth century, the great Indian scholar Vasubandhu, who is seen as a founder of the Mind Only school, and a patriarch of Zen, held that mantras are meaningless gibberish. The idea of mantras offends the spirit of Buddhist logic, which is supposed to be free of superstition. A leads to B, and B leads to C. There's a list of six kinds of A, and ten kinds of B. That's it. No need for magic charms.

Even mystically inclined commentators in later centuries such as Kukai in Japan, and Vajrapani in India, were worried about the mantra because it doesn't quite fit. A sutra is supposed to explain an idea, while a mantra is a magical charm. Does the mantra in the Heart Sutra mean something, in which case it's a 'revealed' teaching that anyone could understand, or is it an occult mystery that only a few initiates could grasp, in which case it's a 'hidden' secret?

Kukai, trying to explain how the revealed and the hidden could co-exist, wrote: 'Revealed and hidden – it depends on the reader. It is not a matter of sounds and letters. There is the hidden within the revealed. And within the hidden, there's the more deeply hidden. Shallow and profound are multilayered.' He adds: 'In the eyes of a great physician, a plant by the wayside is medicine. To a man who knows jewels, in a rock he sees gemstones.'

By the twentieth century, hocus pocus like mantras was no longer well accepted, especially in the West. D. T. Suzuki, the legendary introducer of Zen to America in the early twentieth century, was offended by the existence of mantras, which he felt were completely useless. He thought that the *dharani* in the Lankavatara Sutra, *'Tutte tutte vutte vutte'*, was especially ridiculous, calling it an 'abnormality in religious symbology'. As for the mantra in the Heart Sutra, Suzuki dismissed it as 'apparently a degradation or a degeneration', adding that the mantra 'taken in itself has no meaning, and its vital relation to the *Prajnaparamita* is unintelligible'. He asks with exasperation: 'What is the meaning of this abrupt transformation? Why this nonsense, so to speak?'

Love it or hate it, the mantra has fuelled quite an emotional debate. In Suzuki's day, it was vital to get rid of the superstitious element in order to introduce Zen to the rational West. Even Japan, which was rapidly modernizing, wanted no part of this voodoo.

Most modern commentators treat the mantra very carefully, like people in protective white suits wearing lead gloves as they handle radioactive material. In their zeal to transfer the emphasis from mantic power to philosophy, they do to the mantra what Xuanzang said should never be done – they translate it.

Hakuin, with his usual flash of irreverent insight, shoots right past the words of mantra. He says simply, ' Cherish the great mantra of your own nature.'

能除一切苦

No jo issai ku – With it one escapes all suffering

The sutra says that if you recite this mantra you will escape all suffering. But, we are in fact supposed to feel the suffering of other people. That's 'compassion', which is the result and companion of wisdom. As the Dalai Lama says: 'The mind which cherishes other sentient beings more than oneself, is the pillar of the bodhisattva's practice.'

That's why, at the end of the Ten Bull Pictures, the sage re-enters the market place. He has work to do. We've come full circle to the beginning of the sutra, back to *gyo* ('practice'). One begins to see why Kuiji, the first commentator, devoted a third of his book to practice. Once you start feeling compassion, you end up going in precisely the opposite direction from what the sutra promises – far from escaping suffering, you take on more.

The paradox remains – in the Heart Sutra, you just can't get around it – that the kindness to others that is mandated to us as human beings means next to nothing in the light of the eternal. Nagarjuna once wrote: 'The Bodhisattva aims to save all sentient beings, but the Bodhisattva sees no sentient beings.'

Jasper Griffin, a classics professor who taught at Balliol College in my student days, used to say, with the sharp wit of an old-style Oxford don: 'Compassion is human. Sympathy, angelic. Apathy, divine.'

'Apathy' may sound rather cold, but it's good advice for a bodhisattva. There are times when showing sorrow and offering understanding are the very best things we can do for others. But sadness, all by itself, can do nothing. Bodhisattvas know that the means available to them are limited, and life with its griefs will mostly go on regardless. So, undisturbed by tragedy and failure, they do their job with a minimum of fuss, never losing that faint Buddha smile on their lips. True compassion keeps a distance, is removed, even humorous, as David Kidd or Gilkey used to be. Proust's narrator observes:

> Whenever in the course of my life I have come across, in convents for instance, truly saintly embodiments of practical charity, they have generally had the cheerful, positive, brusque and unemotioned air of a busy surgeon, the sort of face in which one can discern no commiseration, no tenderness at the sight of suffering humanity, no fear of hurting it, the impassive, unsympathetic, sublime face of true goodness.

真実不虚

Shinjitsu fu ko – It is truth and reality, without falsehood

The Heart Sutra is merciless in the way that it slices away absolutely everything. It's so clean and swift you barely feel it. The flash of realization that comes with the Heart Sutra can be devastating, though it may take years before you realize you've been sliced. Hanshan Deqing sums it up: '*Hannya* is like a sword that cuts all things which touch it so sharply that they do not know they are cut. Who but sages and saints can make use of it? Certainly not the ignorant!'

Diane Barraclough once commented on David Kidd's slashing wit: 'The thing is, with David you felt the excruciating pain immediately. Sometimes he struck at random, because he just couldn't resist a clever remark. That's when it really hurt. But other times his words were liberating. They released you, they cut away something you should be free from.' If Gilkey represented the wisdom of Manjusri, then David was Manjusri's flashing sword.

In my old house in Iya Valley, where the iron kettle dangled from a 'freely hanging' piece of bamboo, after centuries of smoke rising from the floor-hearth, everything – the walls, columns, even the floors – had turned pitch black. Outside the house on a winter night it was even darker on the steep hillsides. In that black-floored and black-walled room, when visitors came, we would stay up late telling ghost stories around the hearth. One of these was about the Scythe Weasel. To this day I remember the Scythe Weasel when I find myself alone at night on one of Iya's mountain paths.

The story goes that a man on a journey stops at night at an inn in the countryside. People tell him he is lucky to have escaped the Scythe Weasel. He says, 'Well, there might be something out there, but I wouldn't worry about it. After dark as I was walking along the path, I saw a flash of light and heard what could have been a shriek. But that's it.'

He sits down by the fire, and then they notice a thin red line running from his right shoulder to his left hip. Noiselessly the two halves of his body slip apart.

PART 10

The Chant

故説、 般若波羅蜜多呪。	Therefore we chant the mantra of *Hannya Haramita*.
即説呪曰、	Now we chant, saying:
羯諦羯諦、	*Gyatei gyatei,*
波羅羯諦、	*Hara gyatei,*
波羅僧羯諦、	*Hara so gyatei,*
菩提薩婆訶。	*Bodai sowaka.*
般若心経	Heart of Wisdom Sutra

The last part, where we chant the sutra, is often described by commentators as the attainment of pure wisdom. But actually, this is where we leave wisdom behind.

In the early seventeenth century, Hanshan Deqing recognized that the mantra is a call to action: 'It has already been called *hannya* [wisdom], why is it also called mantra? This is to show the speed of its supernatural efficacy. It's like a secret order from army central command. If you can execute it discreetly, you will never fail to achieve victory.'

In this book, I've taken the step – standard for a thousand years, but radical in this day and age – of treating the mantra as an engine of magical power. But I find myself wondering what possible use the mantra could be to rational modern people, who reserve that stuff for Harry Potter and not for real life.

In fact, many if not most of the people who recite the sutra nowadays treat the mantra not so much as a magic charm, but as a 'daily affirmation'. In ancient Sanskrit, there was the concept of a *gatha*, a verse which when chanted would lead one to mindfulness. In recent years, Thich Nhat Hanh has popularized *gathas*, creating songs and poems for picking flowers, washing the dishes, even sitting on the toilet. You recite a *gatha* as you breathe in and out in preparation for a meditation.

You can chant the Heart Sutra mantra as a *gatha*, a personal ritual lifting your heart out of the day-to-day. Or, like Domo Geshe reciting the *Yiggya*, you can chant the mantra because it works.

故説

Ko setsu – Therefore we chant

The sutra says, 'Therefore we chant,' but you don't need to say the sutra out loud. The word 'chant' might be better translated as 'express' or 'broadcast', since you can also write it.

Calligraphy has been my way to 'chant' the sutra, usually in the company of an old friend. Talking, laughing and drinking many glasses of red wine, we work our way through sheet after sheet, character after character. I find myself writing 心 ('Heart'), 般若 (*'Hannya'*), 咒 (*'Mantra'*), and other words from the Heart Sutra. And especially, of course, 色即是空 ('The material world is itself emptiness').

At that first encounter when Zen monk Urata waved around his fan, what intrigued me was not the meaning of the chant, of which I had no idea, but the script on the fan, inscribed in gold on a dark blue ground. It turns out that gold-on-blue has a long history, dating back to Heian nobles when they copied out the Heart Sutra on luxurious blue-dyed papers back in the tenth century. That's why Urata's fan was blue, and so was Yourcenar's, and so is my Heart Sutra necktie.

Ever since then, I have devoted myself to writing the sutra rather than speaking it. This is hardly unusual – I'm following a tradition of sutra-copying known as *shakyo* 写経. Where *shakyo* takes a different path from regular calligraphy is that when you write a character, it is not just a word. It's a buddha. You sometimes see old Heart Sutra *shakyo* manuscripts, in which every character sits on a drawing of a little lotus throne, just like a buddha. There's even a tradition of practice called 'One Character, Three Bows', in which you bow and raise your hands in prayer three times before writing each word. It's because, as Kukai says: 'Each letter contains limitless meanings, and each dot holds infinite truths.'

You can copy the sutra, as Heian princesses used to do, with delicate calligraphy in gold ink arranged in neatly aligned columns on a blue handscroll. Or you can use a big brush, which is my preferred way, and scrawl the characters one by one on large sheets of paper. Kukai, who was famed as a calligrapher, used the metaphor of brush and ink for his ultimate vision of the Heart Sutra:

> Inscribed with the brush of Mount Sumeru, and the ink
>   of the Seas,
> Heaven-and-earth itself is the sutra book.

Typically, *shakyo*, as it is performed in temples in Japan, is a serious business. People sit at low desks and write with total concentration. In fact, it's taught that 'concentration' is one of the virtues you can learn from *shakyo*. But I follow no particular ritual as I write, drinking plenty of wine and chatting with my friend until dawn.

般若波羅蜜多咒

Hannya Haramita shu – The mantra of Hannya Haramita

You can chant it, you can write it as calligraphy, or you can just blow the mantra into the air.

Across Asia there's the belief that turning a wheel with sutras in it whirls their protective power into the sky and across the world. Certain temples in Japan and China have special 'sutra-turning halls'. In the centre of the hall stands a hexagonal sutra library, sometimes itself the size of a small building, constructed around a pillar fitted to a hole in the ceiling and a hole in the floor. If you push one of the hexagonal corners, the sutra library swivels around the pillar, and out from it flows merit to yourself and others.

In Tibet, rows of prayer wheels surround temples, and devotees walk alongside rolling each one as they go. There are also small portable prayer wheels that pilgrims carry in one hand, with a little weight at the end of a fly-string tied to the wheel, making it easy to spin as you walk. Or you can string up flags printed with sutra texts, hang them in the mountains and let the wind waft the sutra wisdom into the wilderness. Rows and rows of prayer flags flapping in the wind over valleys and mountain passes are a common sight in Tibet and Bhutan.

In Japan, at certain special rituals, you see monks reading from huge stacks of sutras, which typically take the shape of long narrow booklets bound accordion-style. After reading a few words, a monk will flip the booklet through his hands, the accordion pages swishing in a high-flowing arc, before he closes it up again. In doing so, he has 'chanted' the book, and now he turns to the next one. This practice is called *tendoku*, 'turnover reading' or 'flipover reading'. It's a way to get through a lot of sutras without spending all day.

Certain sects hold annual *Hannya Tendoku*, in which they read the entire long edition of the 'Long *Hannya Haramita* Sutra', of which the Heart Sutra is the digest version. That's 100,000 lines. Rather than read from each sutra book, they chant an invocation to *ku* ('emptiness') as they flip through the sutras. It goes:

内空外空。内外空。空空。大空。
勝義空。有為空。無為空。畢竟空。
無際空。散空。無変異空。本性空。
自相空。共相空。一切法空。不可得空。
無性空。自性空。無性自性空。

Inner *ku*, Outer *ku*, Inner and Outer *ku*, *Ku ku*, Great *ku*,
Highest Principle *ku*, Action *ku*, Inaction *ku*, Absolute *ku*,
Infinite *ku*, Dissolving *ku*, Unchanging *ku*, True Nature *ku*,
Individual *ku*, General *ku*, All *Dharma ku*, Unattainable *ku*,
Non-self *ku*, Self *ku*, Non-self and Self *ku*.

In case someone could have any doubt about what is the main theme of *Hannya Haramita*, this should certainly clinch it. While they are chanting, the sutra books fold and unfold in rippling waves through their hands, creating a palpable breeze. They call this the '*Hannya Haramita* wind'.

But anyway, what's really so sacred about the verses of the Heart Sutra and its mantra? Maybe other sounds would have done just as well. About the sutra's many repetitions of the word 'mantra', Hakuin comments: 'It keeps talking about it over and over. What about woodcutters' songs? Fishermen's chants? Where do they come in? What about warbling thrushes and twittering swallows?'

即説呪曰

Soku setsu shu watsu – Now we chant, saying

The purpose of chanting the mantra is to awaken its magic power. However, magic powers like this are called *siddhi*, and they are notoriously unreliable. While it could quite possibly transform the world, magic is most often used for essentially trivial activities, like keeping laundry dry. Also, 'mind-painting' power is very tempting to misuse.

A: I think it might be easier to put the dark on someone than the light.

G: Besides, it's kind of fun. Black requires less power than white. That's why black magicians, evil enchantresses, even ordinary people with resentments wield the power they do. So you should never antagonize a mage. He might curse you. Of course he shouldn't, but he might.

A: Gilkey, stop that!

G: Well, he might, that's all.

At one point during our occult investigations, Gilkey and I put together a little 'grimoire', a magician's notebook. It had to do with how you can change the world through the power of thought, and I called it 'The Fifty Laws of Magic'.

The Buddha had warned against getting caught up in *siddhi*, which rarely do us any good. Tibetan lore speaks of a sage who could stop the sun by pointing at it with his finger, yet could not pay his wine bill. Figuring out the laws and putting that book together was a great pleasure, but then Gilkey and I thought of the danger of these techniques falling into the wrong hands. So we locked away the 'Fifty Laws' and the book lies hidden in my library to this day. Although I do dip into it now and then.

Whether for good, for ill, or merely trivial, all this talk of magic and mind over matter must rub many modern readers up the wrong way. Certainly David Kidd was of that view. On the one hand, David collected Tibetan art and supported Tibetan lamas. He came to Oomoto because his acupuncturist had convinced him that it was a source of divine healing energy. At the same time, he found Gilkey's studies in spiritualism to be a quaint foible in his old friend. Once, after listening to Gilkey expound on some occult concept, David smiled and remarked, 'You're suffering from a case of transcendental gullibility.'

Even Gilkey had his doubts. He said, 'You have your bad days when you think, "I am really dreaming up a pot of porridge, and to hell with it."'

羯諦羯諦

Gyatei, gyatei – 'Passing, passed'

Now we say the mantra.

Gyatei, gyatei is the Sino-Japanese rendering of Sanskrit *gate, gate*, pronounced 'latte, latte'. The usual translation of *gate, gate* is 'going, gone', 'passing, passed' announcing that you have reached the end of your voyage across the sea in the vessel of the Heart Sutra, and are finally arriving at the other side.

Fazang, with his eye for detail, points out that there are two *gate, gate*, not just one. It's got to do with compassion, the wish to save others as well as ourselves. Fazang says that the first *gate* is for us, and the second one is to help others.

Mantra sceptics are not entirely happy with such explanations. Sheng Yen, one of the twentieth century's prominent Chinese Zen masters, wrote a book on the Heart Sutra in which he says: 'the last line ("*Gate, Gate*, etc."), is not a true mantra, though it is in the form of a mantra . . . Although mantras can have rich and varied meanings, they are usually not specific. And they are usually not translatable.'

It seems that Sheng Yen doesn't like the fact that we know that the Sanskrit words *gate, gate* mean 'going, gone'. He'd prefer that the sounds were more inscrutable. On the other hand, he may be overestimating how understandable it is.

One night at David Kidd's house, he brought out a large Tibetan painting, which was mostly pitch black. Within the blackness floated objects outlined in gold – hatchets, strings of jewels, crowns and so on. Kalsang Rinpoche, who happened to be there, informed us that the viewer is supposed to fill in the missing images. If you have meditated long enough, you will be able to see wrathful gods or beneficent goddesses bedecked in diadems and necklaces, wielding golden knives and thunderbolts, as they dance and gesticulate in the blackness of the painting.

In the case of *gate, gate*, translations like 'gone beyond' and 'passed' are just the floating ornaments of a ghostly figure hidden in darkness. However, it's not hard to guess who's hidden in the dark painting of the Heart Sutra mantra. There's a fragrance emanating from those words, which Osho had called 'the sweetness of nothingness', a telltale scent giving away her divine presence.

The '*-e*' ending in Sanskrit is feminine, which is to say, that *gate* refers to a woman. The same was true for the long mantra in the Lankavatara Sutra, the one that D. T. Suzuki so objected to that runs '*Tutte tutte vutte vutte patte patte katte katte*' and so on. That also was addressed to a woman, that is, a goddess. So the true translation of *gate, gate* is '*she* is going, *she* has gone'.

The 'she' of the Heart Sutra is, of course, the goddess Hannya Haramita. If we were initiated, we would have been able to see her face and body emerging from behind the words. Wisdom, Mother of the Buddhas, has been with us all along. Now she reappears to welcome us to the other side.

波羅羯諦

Hara gyatei – 'Passed to the other shore'

The *hara* of *Hara gyatei* is the same as the *hara* in *haramita*, meaning 'other shore'. So this line means: 'Passed to the other shore'.

Altogether the mantra consists of just four lines:

Gyatei, gyatei,
Hara gyatei,
Hara so gyatei,
Bodai sowaka.

The commentators say that different people require more or less detail in order to penetrate to the deep meaning of *Hannya Haramita*. That's why we needed versions of 100,000, 25,000 and 8,000 lines.

The Heart Sutra, with less than sixty lines, would seem to be the minimum, but actually there's an even shorter version. It is the mantra at the end, which we are now chanting, that contains within just four lines all the power and insight of the preceding lines. Fazang and Kukai stressed that the reciting of the mantra sums up the sutra itself.

But even this can be shortened. One version of the Heart Sutra exists in Tibet and Japanese Shingon that consists of just a single syllable, *Ah*. Another version, known as the Sutra of Perfect Wisdom in One Letter, compresses the text into the single sound *Om*. *Ah* and *Om*, alpha and omega, are the beginning and end of all things.

If you seek the profound essence that precedes even these, you'll have to make the long journey to the west to Buddha's citadel. There, deep in the library, Ananda and Kasyapa are still guarding the sutras that were not given to Monkey, Pig and Xuanzang to take back to the world. They're the original true sutras, and they have no words at all.

波羅僧羯諦

Hara so gyatei – 'We have all passed'

This is the moment of arrival at the other shore.

D. T. Suzuki, resistant to the idea of mystical power, was troubled by the mantra. After giving it much thought, he came to the conclusion that the mantra sums up the moment of enlightenment – it's a shout of joy. He writes: 'Utterly exhausted intellectually and emotionally, Kannon made a final leap. The last tie which had held him to the world of relativity and "self-power" completely snapped. He found himself on the other shore. Overwhelmed with his feelings, he could only keep uttering *"Gate!"* The *"Gate!"* then became his mantra, the *"Gate!"* became the mantra of the *Prajnaparamita*.'

From a personal point of view, I find less joy and more sadness, Japanese-style *mono-no-aware*, in this line, 'We have all passed'. The 'other shore' is death, nirvana, nothingness. It's the dark shore where I am headed, along with everyone else.

The mood recalls a nineteenth-century painting called the *Isle of the Dead*, by Arnold Böcklin, which inspired Rachmaninoff, Strindberg and Salvador Dali. In it, a white-robed figure is standing in a boat, hooded, with his back to us, as an oarsman draws him towards an island with tall rocky cliffs and dark cypresses. There's a sense of foreboding and finality. You know that when the boat reaches the island, it's all over. Suzuki thinks of the other shore in the sutra as a place to jump for joy. In my darker moments, I think of it as the grim Isle of the Dead.

But then I look back at what those who have meditated on this sutra for a thousand years have said. For them, the other shore is neither white, black nor grey; it's not joyful and not sad. It's immaterial, invisible, beyond absolutely everything; it's the air above the pagoda's spire, the umbrellas of pure spirituality spreading out from the peak of Mount Sumeru.

Mother Hannya Haramita waits up there in the clear emptiness to gather us back into her embrace.

菩提薩婆訶

Bodai sowaka – 'To purest enlightenment'

The Chinese and Japanese versions end with this phrase. *Bodai*, which is *bodhi* in Sanskrit, means 'enlightenment', and *sowaka* is the Sanskrit *svaha*, which means 'purest'. It can also mean 'hail to', or as Kazuaki Tanahashi interprets it, 'blessings to'.

Those are the accepted meanings of *sowaka*, but Fazang had his own take on this word. According to him, '*Sowaka* means "Speed." It's because we wish to reach the other side as fast as possible.' There's no accounting for how Fazang came up with his definition of 'speed'. However, Fazang was not only a Buddhist philosopher, but a magician, whose cabalistic powers won over the Empress Wu. As a master of mystical learning, he seems to have been privy to knowledge we don't have today, and he certainly has a knack of picking out the unexpected secrets of things.

'Speed' brings us back to the fact of the Heart Sutra's extreme shortness. It's all over in a flash. Before we know it, we're crossing the finishing line. There's no time to linger. Look away and you'll miss something. We began the Heart Sutra with a breathless run, and we're still sprinting as we reach the end.

As in our own short lives.

般若心経

Hannya Shingyo – Heart of Wisdom Sutra

While the Japanese and Chinese versions conclude with *sowaka*, the Tibetan version is not in such a hurry, and continues on to a festive finale.

The scene reverts to Vulture Peak where the bodhisattva Kannon (also known as Avalokiteshvara) has been addressing Shariputra on behalf of the Buddha. At this point the Buddha arises from deep meditation and praises Avalokiteshvara for a job well done. The sutra ends with this joyful line:

> As the Blessed One uttered these words, the venerable Shariputra, the holy Avalokiteshvara (the bodhisattva, the great being), along with the entire assembly, including the worlds of gods, humans, demigods, and heavenly musicians, all rejoiced and hailed what the Blessed One had said.

The fifteenth-century Tibetan monk Jamyang Gawai Lodrö captures the mood of celebration, writing: 'After reciting this mantra if one exclaims the power of its truth and claps their hands, one will receive great waves of blessing.'

Glossary of Terms

While I've tried to explain Buddhist terms and related topics when they first appear in the book, I thought it might be helpful to list them together as an aid for anyone interested in learning more about the concepts underlying the Heart Sutra. Cross-references to other entries, both here and in 'People Mentioned in the Text' (pp. 267–75), are highlighted in bold. The following abbreviations are used: (C) = Chinese; (J) = Japanese; (S) = Sanskrit; (Tb) = Tibetan; (Th) = Thai.

Ah (S) The first sound, the beginning of all things. Paired with *Om*.

Alaya (S) 阿賴耶識 'Storehouse Consciousness'.

anatta (S) Buddhist doctrine that there is no unchanging or permanent soul.

atappa (S), (J) *yumo* 勇猛 'Ardency' or 'engagement'.

Blue Cliff Record (J) *Hekiganroku*「碧巖録」A collection of Zen **koans**, compiled around AD 1135 in China.

bodai (S) Enlightenment.

bodhicitta (S), (J) *busshin* 仏心 'Buddha heart'. The desire to seek enlightenment and be compassionate, also known as 'buddha nature'.

bodhisattva (S) An enlightened being who makes a vow to save all sentient beings.

bonno (J) 煩悩 'Distracting thoughts' – beauty, fear, envy, wealth, etc.

buddha heart See *bodhicitta*.

Causes of Suffering (J) *jittai* 集諦 Second of the **Four Noble Truths**: desire and its consequences. In the Heart Sutra, abbreviated to the single character *shu* 集.

Cessation of Suffering (J) *mettai* 滅諦 Third of the **Four Noble Truths**: giving up desire. In the Heart Sutra, abbreviated to the single character *metsu* 滅.

Chang'an (C) 長安 Capital of **Tang dynasty** China.

citta See **heart**.

Daisen-in (J) 大仙院 Sub-temple of **Daitokuji**.

Daitokuji (J) 大徳寺 Important Zen temple in Kyoto.

dharani (S), (J) *darani* 陀羅尼 Alternative word for **mantra**.

dharma (S), (C) *ho* 法 'Law'. The term *dharmas* (small *d*) refers to the natural rules and logic that determine how things are. As 'the *Dharma*' (capital *D*), it refers to the **Buddha**'s teachings.

Edo period (1603–1868). Period of feudal rule in Japan by the Tokugawa shoguns based in Edo (which became Tokyo after 1868).

Enchiridion A handbook of the sayings of the Greek Stoic philosopher Epictetus (*c*. AD 50–135), compiled by his disciple Arrian (*c*. AD 86–*c*.146), stressing self-reliance.

End of the *Dharma* (J) *mappo* 末法 A degenerate age in which the **Buddha**'s teachings are no longer listened to and apocalypse approaches.

equanimity One of the Six (or Ten) Perfections, called *upekkha* in Pali, *upeksha* in Sanskrit and *sha* 捨 in Japanese.

evam See **nyoze**.

Five Baskets (S) *skandhas*, (J) *go-on* 五蘊 The five ways in which we perceive or engage with the world around us: 色 the Material World, 受 Sensation, 想 Thought, 行 Action and 識 Consciousness.

Flower Garland Sutra (S) *Avamtasaka Sutra*, (J) *Kegonkyo*「華厳経」 A Buddhist sutra which stresses the interconnectivity of all things.

Four Major Sufferings Birth, old age, illness, death.

Four Minor Sufferings Parting from loved ones, cohabiting with people you can't stand, failure to get what you want, physical discomfort.

Four Noble Truths (J) *shitai* 四諦: (1) **Suffering**; (2) **Causes of Suffering**; (3) **Cessation of Suffering**; (4) the **Noble Way**.

fu (J) 不 'Not'.

gan (J) 願 'Wish', in particular the wish for salvation.

gate, gate (S), (J) *gyatei, gyatei* 羯諦羯諦 'Going, gone', 'passing, passed'. Part of the mantra at the end of the Heart Sutra.

The Gateless Barrier (J) *Mumonkan* 「無門関」 A thirteenth-century collection of forty-eight Zen **koans** by the Chinese Zen master **Wumen Huikai** (Mumon Ekai in Japanese).

gatha (S), (J) *geju* 偈頌 A song or poem that leads to mindfulness.

Gion Shoja (J) 祇園精舍 The Jetavana Monastery in India, where **Buddha** gave many of his sermons.

gyatei, gyatei See *gate, gate*.

gyo (J) 行 'Practise' or 'practice', as in spiritual practice; also 'to go'.

Hamsa bird (S) An ancient Hindu symbol, this is a legendary bird similar to a goose or swan. In Buddhism it became associated with **Shakyamuni**.

hannya (J) 般若 'Wisdom', the Japanese reading of Sanskrit *prajna*.

haramita (J) 波羅蜜多 'Perfection', the Japanese reading of Sanskrit *paramita*.

heart (S) *citta*, (J) *shin* 心 It can mean both 'heart' and 'mind'.

Heian period (J) Japanese historical period (794–1185), characterized by rule by elegant nobles.

Heisenberg uncertainty principle A principle of quantum theory postulating that certain pairs of attributes of subatomic particles can never be known with certainty, such as position and momentum.

Himmaphan (Th) In the *Traiphum* cosmology, the sacred forest at the border between the human world and the world of spirituality, filled with weird and wonderful beings.

hossu (J) 払子 'Whisk', symbolic of brushing away the flies of care.

i (J) 意 (pronounced 'ee'). 'Mind', 'intent' and, by extension, 'ego'.

I Ching (C) or *Yi-jing* 「易経」 'Book of Changes'. Chinese book of divination, compiled between 1000 and 200 BC.

Indra's Net A metaphor in the **Flower Garland Sutra**. **Indra**, Lord of the Universe, has an infinite net, at each knot of which is a jewel, which reflects every other jewel.

Isle of the Dead A painting (1880–86) by Swiss symbolist artist Arnold Böcklin (1827–1901).

jizai (J) 自在 'Freely', translation of Sanskrit *ishvara*, meaning 'free', and also 'mighty', an epithet for **Shiva**.

Journey to the West (C) *Xiyouji* 「西遊記」 Chinese novel by Wu Cheng'en (1500–1582), published in 1592, about the travels to India of **Xuanzang** and his loyal companions Pig and Monkey in search of Buddhist **sutras**.

Kalachakra (Tb) The 'Wheel of Time'. It signifies both the cycles of history and of internal realization.

kanji (J) Japanese writing characters, derived from Chinese.

karma (S) The spiritual principle of cause and effect leading to one's circumstances in life. It can also mean 'fate'.

kang (C) 炕 A large, bed-sized Chinese sofa or throne usually made of carved wood.

ke (J) 罣 The first character of the compound *kege* 罣礙, meaning 'encumbrance'.

koan (J) 公案 An impossible question used in Zen meditation to force the student's mind to go beyond normal rational categories.

ku (J) 空 'Emptiness'. The Japanese reading of Sanskrit **sunyata**.

Lankavatara Sutra (S), (J) *Ryogakyo* 「楞伽経」'Scripture of the Descent into Lanka'. A **sutra** important to Zen, propounding **Mind Only** teachings.

Lotus Sutra (J) *Myoho rengekyo* 「妙法蓮華経」One of the most popular and influential Mahayana sutras, the basis of Tendai and Nichiren Buddhism in Japan.

Mahayana One of the two large divisions of Buddhism, the other being **Theravada**. Today it predominates in China and Tibet, Vietnam, Korea, Mongolia and Japan. In contrast to Theravada, it incorporates teachings that sprang up after the death of **Shakyamuni**, such as the concept of the **bodhisattva**.

Mandelbrot set Named after French mathematician Benoit Mandelbrot (1924–2010), known for his work on fractals, this comprises a set of numbers plotted on the two axes of the 'complex plane' (one axis to show the 'real' part of a number and the other the 'imaginary' part), which reveal ever-finer recursive detail at increasing degrees of magnification.

Man'yoshu (J) 「万葉集」'Collection of Ten Thousand Leaves'. Japan's oldest poetry anthology, compiled after A D 759.

mantra (S), (J) *shu* 呪 Consisting of sacred syllables used as a mystical chant, often found within a **sutra**.

McAllister's Sniff The principle that when we get up close, we can't resist taking a look at, or a sniff of, the thing we most loathe. Named after American David McAllister (b. 1950), college classmate of Alex, banker and since 2015 resident in Budapest, Hungary.

merit Buddhist concept that good deeds accrue merit which is applied after death to ensure a better rebirth.

Middle Way (S) A doctrine proposed by the Indian philosopher **Nagarjuna**, according to which there are 'Two Truths': emptiness (*ku*), the higher truth, and the material world (*shiki*), the lower truth, both of which have validity.

miko (J) 巫女 Priestess or shrine maiden in Japanese Shinto; in ancient times, a shamaness.

mind A variant translation of the word *shin* 心 (**heart**). Also used to mean 'consciousness' *shiki* 識, as in the **Mind Only** school.

Mind Only (J) *Yuishiki* 唯識 A school of Buddhism teaching that all things are merely manifestations of mind – which can be interpreted as our individual minds, or as the 'mind of the universe'.

mono-no-aware (J) 物の哀れ Japanese poetic phrase signifying a sense of wonder tinged with sadness at the transience of life.

Mount Sumeru (S), (J) *Shumisen* 須弥山 Regarded in Buddhism as the centre of the universe.

mu (J) 無 'No'.

mudra (S) A symbolic hand gesture.

mujo (J) 無常 Impermanence, transience.

mumyo (J) 無明 Literally 'no light', *mumyo* means ignorance, and hence 'evil'.

naga Mythical serpent-dragon guarding the waters.

Nanzenji (J) 南禅寺 An important Zen temple in Kyoto.

Nicene Creed A statement of Christian belief adopted at the First Council of Nicaea in AD 325.

nirvana (S) A blissful state of 'nothingness' into which the Buddha entered at the time of his death.

Noble Way (J) *dotai* 道諦 Fourth and last of the **Four Noble Truths**, a life of good practice, through which we can reach the transcendent state of **nirvana**. In the Heart Sutra, abbreviated to the single character *do* 道.

nyoze (J) 如是 'Suchness', a direct understanding of the essential quality of absolute reality; ***evam*** in Sanskrit.

Occam's razor A principle of logic proposed by English theologian William of Ockham (or Occam) (1287–1347) that says: 'Entities should not be multiplied without necessity.'

Odic force A spiritualist concept, this is a vital energy, named by Baron Carl von Reichenbach in 1845, that is said to permeate all plants and animals, including humans.

Om (S) The last sound, the end of all things. Paired with *Ah*.

Onsoro (J) 唵蘇魯 A mantra used by **Hakuin**.

Oomoto (J) 大本 A Japanese Shinto 'New Religion' founded in 1892 by spirit writer Deguchi Nao, and further developed by **Onisaburo**.

The Picture of Dorian Gray A novel published in 1890 by the poet and playwright Oscar Wilde (1854–1900) about a hedonistic young man who sinks deeper into degeneration and crime, but never ages. The portrait he keeps in the attic, however, changes to reflect his inner horror.

Prajna (S), (J) *hannya* 般若 'Wisdom'.

Prajna Paramita (S), (J) *Hannya Haramita* 般若波羅蜜多 'Perfection of Wisdom'.

Pure Land Buddhism (J) *Jodoshu* 浄土宗 A belief that through faith in **Amida**, one will find salvation. In Japan, the teachings of **Honen** inspired the Pure Land sect. His disciple **Shinran** founded the **True Pure Land** sect.

Red Cliff Ode (C) *Chibifu* 「赤壁賦」 Poem written in 1082 by Chinese poet-statesman **Su Dongpo** about a trip to the Red Cliffs on the Yangtze River.

rupa (S) 'The material world', translated in Chinese and Japanese as 'colour' 色; see *shiki*.

Ryoanji (J) 龍安寺 Zen temple in Kyoto famed for its sand garden.

sala flowers The flowers blooming on a pair of sala trees beside the Buddha are said to have turned from yellow to white at the time of his death.

samdhya-bhasa (S) 'Twilight language', referring to words or syllables with secret or esoteric meaning.

samsara (S) Literally 'wandering' or 'world', implying constant change. Sometimes translated as 'sea of sorrow' or 'sea of the world'.

samudaya (S), (J) *shu* 集 Literally 'multitude' in Sanskrit, signifying the many **Causes of Suffering**, the second of the **Four Noble Truths**.

Sangha (S) The community of Buddhist followers.

satori (J) 悟 A moment of sudden enlightenment, reached by Zen adepts after practice and meditation.

sha (J) 捨 Literally 'throw away', for Sanskrit *upekkha* (**equanimity**).

shakyo (J) 写経 The tradition of copying **sutras** in beautiful calligraphy, especially the Heart Sutra, as an act of **merit**.

shiki (J) 色 'Colour', for Sanskrit *rupa*, 'the material world'. Also used to mean the sense of 'sight' (what we see with our eyes).

shiki (J) 識 'Mind' or 'consciousness'.

shin (J) 心 See **heart** and **mind**.

shin (J) 真 'Truth'. See the final line of Part 9 of the Heart Sutra: 'It is truth and reality, without falsehood' 「真実不虚」.

Shingon (J) 真言宗 Esoteric Buddhist sect founded by Japanese monk **Kukai**. The word *shingon* means **mantra**.

shu (J) 集 Literally 'collection', Japanese for the Sanskrit *samudaya*.

shu (J) 呪 See **mantra**.

siddhi (S) Magical powers.

Six Sense Organs The six organs with which we take in the world: eyes, ears, nose, tongue, body and mind.

Six Sensory Bases What we perceive with the **Six Sense Organs**: 'colour' (i.e. sight), sound, scent, taste, touch and *dharmas*.

Six Worlds of Perception The knowledge acquired from the **Six Sensory Bases**.

skandhas (S) 'Aggregates' or 'baskets'; see **Five Baskets**.

skilful means (S) *upaya*, (J) *hoben* 方便 The companion to wisdom and compassion.

Song dynasty (C) Chinese dynasty (960–1269).

Sophia The female embodiment of wisdom in the Eastern Orthodox Church.

Soto Zen (J) 曹洞宗 Zen sect introduced from China to Japan by **Dogen** in the thirteenth century. Largest of the Japanese Zen sects, it emphasizes meditation without focus on objects or content.

sowaka (J) 薩婆訶 Japanese for Sanskrit *svaha*, meaning 'purest' or 'hail to'.

Suffering (J) *kutai* 苦諦 First of the **Four Noble Truths**. In the Heart Sutra, abbreviated to the single character *ku* 苦.

sunyata (S), (J) *ku* 空 'Emptiness' propounded by the philosopher **Nagarjuna**, and the principle at the core of the Heart Sutra.

sutra A Buddhist scripture, believed to be the words of the **Buddha**.

Sutra of Perfect Wisdom in One Letter (J) *Ichiji hannya haramita kyo* 「一字般若波羅蜜多経」 A sutra consisting only of one word, the sacred syllable *Om*.

svaha See *sowaka*.

Symposium Written by Plato in *c.*385–370 BC as one of his dialogues, this relates the conversation during a banquet at which the philosopher **Socrates** and other guests discuss love and beauty.

The Tale of the Heike (J) *Heike monogatari* 「平家物語」 Japanese epic (*c.*1300) about the fall of the Heike clan in the late twelfth century.

Tang dynasty (C) Chinese dynasty (618–907).

Ten Bull Pictures (J) *Jugyuzu* 十牛図 Originating in China in the twelfth century, a set of short poems accompanied by images that describe the stages on the pathway to enlightenment.

Tendai Buddhism (J) *Tendaishu* 天台宗 A sect of Esoteric Buddhism introduced from China to Japan in the early ninth century by the monk **Saicho**.

tendoku (J) 転読 A way of speed-chanting long books of **sutras** while flipping their pages through the air.

terton (Tb) A treasure seeker who discovers 'hidden teachings'.

tetralemma A form of logic in four parts used in ancient India. In Sanskrit called *catuskoti*, meaning 'four corners'.

Theravada One of the two large divisions of Buddhism, the other being **Mahayana**. Today it predominates in Thailand, Cambodia, Laos, Myanmar and Sri Lanka. In contrast to Mahayana, Theravada remains closer to the Buddhism preached by **Shakyamuni** during his lifetime.

Tower of Maitreya (S) Tower to which the hero of the **Flower Garland Sutra** is led by **Maitreya**, within which he sees an infinity of worlds reflecting each other.

Traiphum (Th) 'Three Worlds' cosmology, compiled in Thailand in the fourteenth century, describing three worlds of ascending spirituality, centred on **Mount Sumeru**.

True Pure Land Buddhism (J) *Jodo Shinshu* 浄土真宗 A sect of Japanese Buddhism based on the teachings of **Shinran**, this is an offshoot of **Pure Land Buddhism**. It believes that salvation lies in faith in **Amida**.

Twelve Links of Dependent Origination Ignorance, action, consciousness, the six senses, sense impressions, feelings, desire, attachment, becoming, birth, old age and death.

Two Truths See **Middle Way**.

upaya See **skilful means**.

upekkha See **equanimity**.

vajra (S), (J) *kongo* 金剛 A Buddhist ritual implement in the shape of a sceptre with two ends that may be rounded, or sharp like a weapon; symbol of adamantine power.

Vajra **Sliver** A technique in Tibetan logic by which all inessential elements are chopped away.

Venus of Willendorf A prehistoric female figurine dated to *c.*35000 BC, found near Willendorf in Austria.

Vulture Peak The mountaintop in what is now Rajgir, India, where the Buddha gave many of his lectures.

Western Paradise (J) *Saiho gokuraku jodo* 西方極楽浄土 In **Pure Land** and **True Pure Land Buddhism**, the paradise where **Amida** resides and where he brings the souls of those who have had faith in him.

World Beyond Form (Th) *Arupa Phum*, the highest world in the *Traiphum*.

World of Form (Th) *Rupa Phum*, the middle world in the *Traiphum*.

World of Sensuality (Th) *Kama Phum*, the lowest world in the *Traiphum*.

Yiggya (Tb) A hundred-syllable Tibetan **mantra** devoted to Vajrasattva, the god who clears obstructions to spiritual advance.

People Mentioned in the Text

Cross-references to other entries, both here and in the 'Glossary of Terms' (pp. 255–66), are highlighted in bold. The following abbreviations are used: (C) = Chinese; (J) = Japanese; (S) = Sanskrit; (Tb) = Tibetan; (Th) = Thai.

Amida (J) 阿弥陀仏 or 阿弥陀如来 **Buddha** of the **Western Paradise**.

Amranand, Ping. Thai student who attended the Oomoto Seminar in the 1970s.

Ananda (S) (fifth/fourth century BC). First of the disciples of the **Gautama Buddha** and the one entrusted with the **sutras** after his death.

Astrologo, Marina (active since 1977). Italian interpreter and translator of literary works from Gore Vidal to J. K. Rowling.

Avalokiteshvara See **Kannon**.

Barraclough, Diane (b. 1960). English educational consultant, based in New York. Diane grew up in Kobe and later lived in Kameoka. She was a friend of **David Kidd** and **William Gilkey**.

Bodhidharma (S) (fourth/fifth century AD). Indian monk who brought Zen from India to China.

Bodhisattva Who Sees Freely (J) Kanjizai Bosatsu 観自在菩薩 Alternative name for **Kannon**.

Boswell, James (1740–95). Younger friend and biographer of **Samuel Johnson**.

Brunnhölzl, Karl (active since 1989). German translator of Tibetan Buddhist texts into English and German; author of *The Heart Attack Sutra* (2012).

Buddha See **Gautama Buddha**.

Confucius (C) Kongzi 孔子 (551 BC–479 BC). Early Chinese humanistic thinker, and founder of 'Confucianism'.

Dalai Lama (Tb) Tenzin Gyatso (b. 1935). The fourteenth Dalai Lama (since 1940), spiritual leader of Tibetan Buddhism, and winner of the Nobel Peace Prize in 1989.

Darikapa (S) (active *c.*1020). Indian mystic and philosopher, and teacher of scholar and mystic Tilopa (988–1069).

Deguchi Naohi (J) 出口直日 (1902–90). Third Spiritual Leader of **Oomoto** (1952–90).

Dendarla Rampa (Tb) (1758–1839). Mongolian lama; author of *Jewel Light Illuminating the Meaning of the Heart Sutra* (*c.*1800).

Dogen (J) Dogen Kigen 道元希玄 (1200–1253). Monk who went to **Song dynasty** China, and brought **Soto Zen** to Japan.

Domo Geshe Rinpoche (Tb) Domo Geshe Rinpoche Ngawang Jigme (1937–2001), Tibetan monk from Sikkim.

Empress Wu (C) 武則天 (624–705). Powerful **Tang dynasty** empress who tried to establish her own new dynasty.

Epictetus. Greek Stoic philosopher (50–135)

Fayan (C) Fayan Wenyi 法眼文益 or Qingliang Wenyi 清涼文益 (d. 958). Creator of a leading school of Chan (Chinese Zen Buddhism).

Fazang (C) 法蔵 (643–712). **Tang dynasty** Buddhist patriarch, magician, and philosopher.

Fo-yin (C) 佛印 (1032–1098). Also known as Zen Master Fo-yin 佛印 禅師, **Song dynasty** monk.

Gautama Buddha (S) (563–483 BC). Also known as Siddhartha Gautama or Shakyamuni, the historical Buddha.

Geshe Sonam Rinchen (Tb) (1933–2013). Tibetan monk and author.

Gilkey, William (1918–99). American pianist and occultist. Born in Chikasha, Oklahoma, he lived in India, China and his later years in Kameoka, Japan.

Griffin, Jasper. Classics professor (1937-2019), who taught at Balliol College, Oxford in Alex's student days.

Gungthang (Tb) Gungthang Rinpoche Könchog Tenpe Drönme (1762–1823). Tibetan monk and author.

Hakuin (J) Hakuin Ekaku 白隠慧鶴 (1686–1768). Major figure in Japanese Zen Buddhism.

Hanshan Deqing (C) 憨山德清 (1546–1623). Chinese monk and poet of the Ming dynasty (1368–1644) who propagated the teachings of Zen and **Pure Land Buddhism**.

Hasunuma Ryochoku (J) 蓮沼良直 (active since 1980s). Prominent Zen monk in Kyoto. Head of administration, Rinzai Zen, **Nanzenji** branch.

Heraclitus (*c.*535–475 BC). Greek philosopher who emphasized constant change as characteristic of the world.

Honen (J) 法然 (1133–1212). Japanese monk (teacher of **Shinran**) who founded the **Pure Land** sect of Japanese Buddhism based on faith in salvation by **Amida**.

Huineng (C) Dajian Huineng 大鑒惠能 (638–713). The Sixth Patriarch of Chan (Chinese Zen Buddhism).

Hyaku Jo (J) 百丈懷海 (Baizhang Huaihai in Chinese) (720–814). A Zen monk who features in Koan 26 of the **koan** anthology *Blue Cliff Record*.

Indra (S) In ancient Hinduism, the Lord of the Universe.

Jamyang Gawai Lodrö (Tb) (1429–1503). Tibetan monk, author of *Thorough Elucidation of the Meaning of the Words: An Exposition of the Heart Sutra*.

Jayarava (active since 1990s). Also known as Michael Attwood, New Zealand-born Buddhist scholar and blogger, living in Cambridge, England.

Johnson, Samuel (1709–84). Essayist, literary critic, editor and author of the first English dictionary. Famed as the 'sage of common sense', he was often called 'Dr Johnson'.

Joshu (J) 趙州 (Zhaozhou in Chinese) (778–897). A Zen monk who features in the Koan 1 in the **koan** anthology *The Gateless Barrier*.

Kalsang Rinpoche (Tb) Rahob Rinpoche Thupten Kalsang (b. *c.*1940). The Sixth Incarnate Abbot of Rahob Monastery in old Tibet. Moved to America in 1979.

Kamalashila (S) (*c.*740–95). Indian philosopher who defeated Chinese Zen monk **Moheyan** in debate at the Council of Lhasa in 792–4.

Kanjizai Bosatsu See **Bodhisattva Who Sees Freely**.

Kannon (J) 観音 or Kanzeon 観世音 Short for Kannon Bosatsu 観音菩薩 ('**bodhisattva** of compassion'), Avalokiteshvara in Sanskrit. See also **Bodhisattva Who Sees Freely**.

Kasyapa (S) (*c.*500 BC). One of the disciples of **Gautama Buddha**.

Kidd, David (1926–96). Art collector and author, resident of Beijing in the 1940s and early 1950s, and later of Ashiya and Kyoto, Japan.

Kuiji (J) 窺基 (632–82). **Xuanzang**'s leading Chinese disciple.

Kukai (J) 空海 (774–835). Monk who travelled from Japan to **Tang dynasty** China, and on his return founded the **Shingon** sect of Esoteric Buddhism.

Kumarajiva (S), (J) Kumaraju 鳩摩羅什 (344–413). Monk translator from the Kingdom of Kucha (in present-day Xinjiang Province of China).

Laozi (C) 老子 (sixth century BC). Legendary early Chinese philosopher and one of the founders of Daoist (Taoist) philosophy.

Lorenz, Edward (1917–2008). American mathematician, meteorologist and a pioneer of chaos theory. He coined the term 'butterfly effect'.

Manjusri (S), (J) Monju Bosatsu 文殊菩薩 The **bodhisattva** of wisdom. He sits on a lion, carrying a book or scroll in one hand, and a flaming sword in the other.

Maitreya (S), (J) Miroku Bosatsu 弥勒菩薩 The Buddha of the Future, sometimes seen as a messiah at the end of times.

Mandelbrot, Benoit. Polish-born French-American mathematician, (1924-2010).

Marvell, Andrew (1621–78). English poet. Author of 'To His Coy Mistress', published posthumously in 1681.

McAllister, David. College friend of Alex, now living in Budapest Hungary (b. 1950)

Mencius (C) Mengzi 孟子 (372–289 BC). Chinese philosopher revered as the 'second Sage' after Confucius.

Moheyan (C) Heshang Moheyan 和尚摩訶衍 (late eighth century). Represented Chan (Chinese Zen) Buddhism in the Council of Lhasa in 792–4, losing to Indian pundit **Kamalashila**.

Mompou, Federico (1893–1987). Spanish impressionist composer.

Munroe, Alexandra (b. 1956). American historian of Asian art and senior curator of Asian Art at the Solomon R. Guggenheim Museum, New York. Friend of **David Kidd**.

Nagarjuna (S) (*c*.150–*c*.250). Mahayana philosopher whose writings centred on the concept of *sunyata*.

Nattier, Jan (active 1980s–2010s). American scholar of Mahayana Buddhism. Author of *The Heart Sutra: A Chinese Apocryphal Text?* (1992).

O'Brien, Barbara (active since 1988). Also known as Barbara Hoetsu O'Brien, Buddhist writer, author of scholarly blogs on *ThoughtCo.com*.

Onisaburo (J) Deguchi Onisaburo 出口王仁三郎 (1871–1948). Co-founder of the Shinto 'New Religion' **Oomoto**.

Osho (1931–90). Also known as Rajneesh, Indian guru who preached meditation and mindfulness.

Otomo no Yakamochi (J) 大伴家持 (*c*.718–785). Japanese poet who features in the eighth-century anthology *Man'yoshu*.

Ozeki Soen (J) 尾関宗園 (b. 1932). Japanese Zen monk and Abbot of **Daisen-in**.

Price, Vincent (1911–93). American movie actor known for his sepulchral voice in film noir and thrillers.

Proust, Marcel. French novelist (1871-1922)

Ramacharaka (1798–1893). Nom de plume of American author and occultist William Walker Atkinson (1862–1932), pioneer of the New Thought movement.

Roberts, Jane Dorothy Jane Roberts (1929–1984). American author and spirit medium who channelled a spirit called 'Seth'.

Saicho (J) 最澄 (767–822). Monk who founded the **Tendai** school of Buddhism in Japan.

Seth See **Roberts, Jane**.

Schrödinger, Erwin (1887–1961). Nobel Prize-winning Austrian-Irish physicist, pioneer of quantum theory.

Shakti (S) Hindu goddess of primordial cosmic energy, often shown in ecstatic union with the god **Shiva**.

Shakyamuni See **Gautama Buddha**.

Shariputra (S), (J) Sharishi 舎利子 (*c*.500 BC). Disciple of **Gautama Buddha**. The Heart Sutra is addressed to him by **Kannon**.

Sheng Yen (C) 聖嚴 (1931–2009). Taiwan-based Chan (Zen) Buddhist master, whose modern approach to Buddhism had an impact upon Europe and America as well as Taiwan.

Shinran (J) 親鸞 (1173–1263). Japanese monk (student of **Honen**), who founded the **True Pure Land** sect of Japanese Buddhism focused on faith in salvation by **Amida**.

Shiva (S) Of the three leading Hindu gods, Shiva is the destroyer. He also creates and transforms the universe. Sometimes he takes the form of Nataraja, the cosmic dancer.

Son, Masayoshi (J) 孫正義 (b. 1957). Korean-Japanese billionaire and technology entrepreneur, founder of SoftBank group of tech companies.

Su Dongpo (C) 蘇東坡 or Su Shi 蘇軾 (1037–1101). Poet and statesman of the **Song dynasty**; author of the *Red Cliff Ode*.

Suzuki, D. T. (J) Suzuki Daisetsu 鈴木大拙 (1870–1966). A pioneer in bringing Zen Buddhism to the West in the twentieth century.

Tachibana Daiki (J) 立花大亀 (1900–2005). Japanese Zen monk and Senior Abbot of **Daitokuji**.

Tamasaburo (J) Bando Tamasaburo 5th 五代目坂東玉三郎 (b. 1950). Kabuki *onnagata* (male player of female roles).

Tanahashi, Kazuaki (J) 棚橋一晃 (b. 1933). Calligrapher and author of *The Heart Sutra: A Comprehensive Guide to the Classic of Mahayana Buddhism* (2016).

Thich Nhat Hanh (b. 1926). Charismatic Vietnamese monk and spiritual leader.

Vajrapani (active eleventh century). Indian master who was instrumental in the transmission of Buddhist texts to Tibet, including the Heart Sutra, on which he wrote a commentary.

Vasubandhu (active fourth/fifth century). Indian Buddhist monk influential in the creation of the **Mind Only** school.

Vimalakirti (S), (J) Yuima Koji 維摩居士 (sixth/fifth century BC). A contemporary of **Shakyamuni**, he was seen as the ideal lay practitioner, famous for his wisdom.

Wallace, B. Alan (b. 1950). American author and expert on Tibetan Buddhism.

Westerhoff, Jan (active since 1999). Author and Professor of Buddhist Philosophy at the University of Oxford.

Woncheuk (Korean) 원측, (J) Enjiki 円測 (613–696). **Xuanzang**'s leading Korean disciple.

Wumen Huikai (C) 無門慧開 (Mumon Ekai in Japanese) (1183–1260). Chinese Zen master and author of *The Gateless Barrier*.

Xin Qiji (C) 辛棄疾 (1140–1207). **Song dynasty** poet and military leader, author of poem '*Chou nu erh*' 「醜奴兒」 about expressing sadness.

Xuanzang (C) 玄奘 or Xuanzang Sanzang 玄奘三藏 (602–64). Monk who travelled to India and brought back to **Tang dynasty** China many **sutras**, including the Heart Sutra, of which he was the first translator.

Yoshida Kenko (J) 吉田兼好 (1284–1350). Japanese author and monk who wrote *Essays in Idleness* (*Tsurezuregusa* 徒然草, 1330–32), about the transience of life.

Yourcenar, Marguerite (1903–87). Belgian-born writer who became a US citizen but continued to write in French. Author of *Memoirs of Hadrian* (1951), and first woman elected to be a member of the Académie Française, in 1980.

Notes

Among the translations cited below there are quotations from a few, notably those of Thomas Eijo Dreitlein (of Kukai), Lu K'wan Yü (of Hanshan Deqing) and Norman Waddell (of Hakuin), which I've altered to some degree based on the original *kanji* (as the characters are called in Japanese). Where edition details aren't provided for a quote in the text (e.g. for *The Tale of the Heike*, or Kenko's *Tsurezuregusa*), it's because the translation is mine.

In the endnotes, most of the quotations based on Chinese or Japanese are also shown in the original *kanji* at the end of a reference. I've done this because I've found it frustrating over the years to read books with English quotes from classical Chinese or Japanese, but not to be able to see the *kanji* and therefore understand the intent of the original. For readers who know these languages, I hope the *kanji* references will be helpful.

Preface

p. 4 'Like the barley . . . to be blamed': Donald S. Lopez Jr, *The Heart Sutra Explained: Indian and Tibetan Commentaries* (Albany, NY: State University of New York Press, 1988), p. 158.

Introduction

p. 13   The records . . . 6,000 scrolls: Guang Xing, 'Buddhist Impact on Chinese Language', *Buddhism Without Borders – Proceedings of the International Conference on Buddhism* (2012), pp. 221–42.

p. 16   'A discussion . . . it teaches': Thomas Eijo Dreitlein (trans.), 'An Annotated Translation of Kūkai's *Secret Key to the Heart Sūtra*', *Bulletin of the Research Institute of Esoteric Buddhist Culture*, vol. 24 (2011), p. 17. 「一一聲字歷劫之談不盡。一一名實塵滴之佛無極。」

Part 1: The Opening

p. 35   'Most folks . . . wisdom': Hakuin, *Zen Words for the Heart: Commentary on the Heart Sutra*, trans. Norman Waddell [*Zen Words for the Heart* is Waddell's rendition of the title of Hakuin's book *Poison Words on the Heart Sutra*] (Boston and London: Shambhala, 2013), p. 7. 「多錯作広博会了 . . . 為我過小底般若来」

p. 38   'The sutras . . . Manjusri': Dreitlein (trans.), 'Kūkai's *Secret Key to the Heart Sūtra*', p. 5, quoting Kukai's *Kongo hannya-haramitsu-kyo kaidai*. 「大般若一部六百卷十六會二百八十二品並是文殊菩薩之三摩地門」

p. 41   'There are things . . . our power': Epictetus, *Enchiridion*, trans. Thomas W. Higginson (New York: Liberal Arts Press, 1948), ch. I.

p. 43   'Stop yelling . . . ones instead': Wu Cheng'en, *Journey to the West*, adapted and revised by Collinson Fair from the 1955 Beijing People's Press Edition, trans. W. J. F. Jenner (Rockville, MD: Silk Pagoda, 2005), pp. 1375–6. 「你如今空手來取、是以

傳了白本。 白本者、乃無字真經、倒也是好的。因你那東土眾
生愚迷不悟、只可以此傳之耳。」

p. 44   *Avalokita* . . . (*kan* 觀 in Chinese): Kazuaki Tanahashi, *The Heart Sutra: A Comprehensive Guide to the Classic of Mahayana Buddhism* (Boulder, CO: Shambala, 2016), p. 148.

p. 45   'To call him . . . his name': Kuiji, *A Comprehensive Commentary on the Heart Sutra*, trans. Heng-ching Shih with Dan Lusthaus (Berkeley, CA: Numata Center for Buddhist Translation and Research, 2001), p. 14. 「但言觀音詞義俱失」

p. 47   'encouragement to practise': Dan Lusthaus, 'The Heart Sutra in Chinese Yogācāra: Some Comparative Comments on the Heart Sutra Commentaries of Wŏnch'ŭk and K'uei-chi', *International Journal of Buddhist Thought & Culture September*, vol. 3 (2003), p. 73.

p. 50   'Rising . . . body golden': Lopez Jr, *The Heart Sutra Explained*, p. 115.

p. 51   'the time has come': Fazang, *Hannya shingyo rakuso* ('Summary of Notes on the Heart Sutra'), trans. Iwata Masanari (Tokyo: Shinjinbutsu Oraisha, 1984), p. 66. 「言時者、謂以此菩薩有時。」

p. 51   'Thus . . . no future': Tanahashi, *The Heart Sutra*, p. 168. 「是空法非過去非未来非現在」

p. 57   'fast-moving boat over stormy seas': Fazang, *Hannya shingyo rakuso*, p. 31. 「済苦海之迅航」

Part 2: The Material World and Emptiness are the Same

p. 67   'if we were walking . . . We are stuck': Geshe Sonam Rinchen, *The Heart Sutra: An Oral Teaching*, ed. Ruth Sonam (Ithaca, NY: Snow Lion Publications, 2003), p. 49.

p. 69 'If you are a poet . . . *inter-are*': Thich Nhat Hanh, *The Other Shore: A New Translation of the Heart Sutra with Commentaries*, rev. edn (Berkeley, CA: Palm Leaves Press, 2017), p. 27.

p. 72 'The sound of the bell . . . the wind': *The Tale of the Heike*. 「祇園精舎の鐘の声、諸行無常の響きあり . . . たけき者もつひには滅びぬ、ひとへに風の前の塵に同じ。」

p. 73 'Song of Grief at the Impermanence of this World': *Man'yoshu*, vol. 19, no. 4160. 「世間の無常を悲しぶる歌」

p. 74 'If the dew . . . most precious': Yoshida Kenko, *Tsurezuregusa* ('Essays in Idleness'), ch. 7. 「あだし野の露消ゆる時なく、鳥部山の煙立ち去らでのみ住みはつる習ひならば、いかにものゝあはれもなからん。世は定めなきこそいみじけれ。」

p. 77 'A nice kettle . . . rat turds': Hakuin, *Zen Words for the Heart*, p. 31. 「好一釜羹被両顆鼠糞汚却」

p. 77 'In all levels . . . humanity needs': Tenzin Gyatso, the Fourteenth Dalai Lama, *Essence of the Heart Sutra: The Dalai Lama's Heart of Wisdom Teachings* (Boston, MA: Wisdom Publications, 2005), p. 7.

p. 78 'Nothingness . . . unclouded': Osho, 'The Fragrance of Nothingness', in his *The Heart Sutra: Talks on Prajnaparamita Hridayam Sutra of Gautama the Buddha* (Pune: Rajneesh Foundation, 1978), p. 65.

p. 78 'The eight winds blow . . . don't move you?': Hsuan Hua, *The Heart of Prajna Paramita Sutra* (Burlingame, CA: Buddhist Text Translation Society, 2002), pp. 30–31.

p. 79 'A monk . . . noble peak': *Blue Cliff Record*, Koan 26. 「僧問百丈如何是奇特事。丈云獨坐大雄峰。」

p. 79 'Sometimes people . . . so what': Andy Warhol, *The Philosophy of Andy Warhol: From A to B and Back Again* (Boston, MA: Houghton Mifflin Harcourt, 2014), p. 112.

p. 82 'the source . . . all marvels': Lopez Jr, *The Heart Sutra Explained*, p. 34.

p. 83 'One should . . . the suchness': Jamyang Gawai Lodrö, *Thorough Elucidation of the Meaning of the Words: An Exposition of the Heart Sutra*, quoted in Tenzin Gyatso, *Essence of the Heart Sutra*, p. 159.

Part 3: The Six Nots

p. 87 'Not arising . . . not going': 「不生不滅、不常不斷、不一不異、不来不去。」

p. 91 'He is planning . . . never write': Marguerite Yourcenar, *Le tour de la prison* (Paris: Gallimard, 1991), p. 129.

p. 93 'like finding . . . high peak': Takeuchi Seiichi, *Hanabira ha chiru, hana ha chiranai – mujo no nihon shiko* (Tokyo: Kadokawa Gakugei Shuppan, 2011), p. 64, quoting Saicho's *Wishes* (*Ganbun*). 「大海の針、妙高の線」

p. 94 'You are an actor . . . another': Epictetus, *Enchiridion*, trans. Higginson, ch. XVII.

p. 96 Nattier figured out . . . ending: Jan Nattier, 'The Heart Sutra: A Chinese Apocryphal Text?', *Journal of the International Association of Buddhist Studies*, vol. 15, no. 2 (1992), pp. 153–223.

p. 97 'People's goodness . . . of water': Mencius, *Mengzi*, vol. 11: *Gaozi*. 「人性之善也，猶水之就下也。 . . . 今夫水搏而躍之，可使過顙，激而行之，可使在山，是豈水之性哉？」

p. 97 'clear-light nature . . . in all of us': Tenzin Gyatso, *Essence of the Heart Sutra*, p. 82.

p. 98 'Basically . . . be attracted?': John McRae, *The Platform Sutra of the Sixth Patriarch* (Berkeley, CA: Numata Center for Buddhist Translation and Research, 2000), p. 33. 「本來無一物。何處惹塵埃？」

p. 99 'We could say . . . last one': Karl Brunnhölzl, *The Heart Attack Sutra: A New Commentary on the Heart Sutra* (Ithaca, NY: Snow Lion Publications, 2012), p. 53.

p. 100 'What is . . . Gate to "Not-Two"': *Blue Cliff Record*, Koan 84.
「何等是菩薩不二法門?」「無言無説、無示無識、離諸問答。
是為不二法門。」

Part 4: No Eyes, Ears, Nose, Tongue, Body or Mind

p. 104 'Never, never, never, never, never!': William Shakespeare,
King Lear, Act V, scene iii.

p. 105 'The sharp sword . . . thoughts': Dreitlein (trans.), 'Kūkai's
Secret Key to the Heart Sūtra', p. 27. 「文殊利劍能揮八不絕彼妄
執之心乎」

p. 109 'The emptiness . . . not endure': Fazang, *Hannya shingyo
rakuso*, p. 27.

p. 109 'As sad . . . fly away': *Man'yoshu*, vol. 5, no 893. 「世間を憂しと
やさしと思へども飛び立ちかねつ鳥にしあらねば」

p. 110 'A Bodhisattva . . . again': Geshe Sonam Rinchen, *The Heart
Sutra*, p. 30.

p. 115 'The history . . . post-mortem continuity': 'There is No Life
After Death, Sorry', *Jayarava's Raves* website, 23 January 2015
(http://jayarava.blogspot.com/2015/01/there-is-no-life-after-
death-sorry.html).

p. 117 'The onus . . . after death': ibid.

p. 120 'Last scene . . . sans everything': William Shakespeare, *As You
Like It*, Act II, scene vii.

p. 121 'But in the course . . . "Where is my horse?"': Osho, 'The
Buddha Within', in his *The Heart Sutra*, pp. 8–9.

p. 121 'The whole process . . . is real': ibid., p. 3.

p. 123 'Respect gods . . . at a distance': Confucius, *Analects*, ch. 6, no. 22.
「敬鬼神而遠之」

p. 126 Darwin, as he pondered . . . 'a taste for the beautiful': On Darwin,
see https://www.nytimes.com/2017/09/18/books/review/

evolution-of-beauty-richard-prum-charles-darwin.html.
On recent research, see Michael Ryan, *A Taste for the Beautiful* (Princeton, NJ: Princeton University Press, 2018) and Richard O. Prum, *The Evolution of Beauty* (New York: Doubleday, 2017).

p. 131 'With mind discriminating . . . all correct': Lusthaus, 'The Heart Sutra in Chinese Yogācāra', p. 59. 「以心分別諸法皆邪。不以心分別諸法皆正。」

p. 131 'And a nose . . . do exist!': Hakuin, *Zen Words for the Heart*, p. 43. 「有眼耳鼻舌身意、有色声香味触法。」

p. 131 'Our intelligence gives us . . . intelligence itself': Tenzin Gyatso, *Essence of the Heart Sutra*, p. 6.

Part 5: No Ageing and No Death

p. 134 'There is P . . . nor not-P': Jan Westerhoff, *History of Philosophy Without Any Gaps*, episode 46, podcast published by King's College London, with Peter Adamson and Jonardon Ganeri, 9 July 2017 (https://historyofphilosophy.net/nagarjuna-tetralemma).

p. 135 'pre-supposition failure': ibid.

p. 139 'A monk asked . . . "*Mu!*"': *The Gateless Gate*, Koan 1. 「趙州和尚因僧問狗子還有佛性也無。州云、無。」

p. 139 'Make your whole body . . . you cannot': Barbara O'Brien, 'What is *Mu*? The Barrier Gate of Zen', *Learn Religions* website (https://www.thoughtco.com/what-is-mu-in-zen-449929, updated 8 March 2017), quoting *The Gateless Gate*, Koan 1. 「將三百六十骨節、八萬四千毫竅、通身起箇疑團參箇無字。晝夜提撕、莫作虛無會、莫作有無會。如吞了箇熱鐵丸相似、吐又吐不出。」

p. 145 'Mind . . . does not create': Imre Hamar, 'The Metaphor of the Painter in the 'Avataṃsaka-sūtra' and Its Chinese Interpretations', SOS 13 · 2 (2014), p. 188 (https://www.academia.edu/13235090). 「心如工畫師 能畫諸世間、五蘊悉從生 無法而不造。」

p. 151 The Mandelbrot set . . . simplest of rules: For a more detailed explanation of the Mandelbrot set, see https://www.youtube.com/watch?v=NGMRB4O922I and for the infinite level of magnification generated by the set, see https://www.youtube.com/watch?v=aSg2Db3jF_4.

p. 152 *'Animula . . . as you used to'*: The poem here is translated from the original Latin. For more on the death of Hadrian and on his poem, with the full Latin text and various translations, including Yourcenar's, see https://followinghadrian.com/2013/07/10/animula-vagula-blandula-hadrians-farewell-to-life/.

p. 155 'Absent . . . well be dead': *Bessatsu taiyo*, special issue on Hakuin (January 2013). 「暫時不在如同死人」

Part 6: *No Noble Way and No Merit*

p. 163 'Suffering and its causes . . . dying': Fazang, *Hannya shingyo rakuso*, p. 142. 「染浄因果門也 。苦集是世間因果。謂苦是生死報。」

p. 164 'Is anything . . . the gods': Epictetus, *Enchiridion*, trans. Higginson, ch. XV.

p. 174 'Let go . . . in his hands': Hakuin, *Zen Words for the Heart*, p. 42. 「放下著抱臟叫屈」

p. 174 'In the Long Wisdom Sutra . . . everything': Fazang, *Hannya shingyo rakuso*, p. 151. 「故大品云、無所得故而得。」

p. 176 when he was young . . . 'The weather is cool, what a lovely autumn': Xin Qiji, *'Chou nu erh'*. 「而今識盡愁滋味, 欲說還休。 欲說還休, 卻道天涼好個秋。」

Part 7: The Heart is Without Encumbrance

p. 183 'There is . . . absolutely precious': Dalai Lama, quoted in Barbara O'Brien, 'Bodhicitta: Practice for the Benefit of All Beings', *Learn Religions* website (https://www.thoughtco.com/teachings-about-bodhicitta-450009, updated 6 March 2017).

p. 185 *'Aak, aak! . . .* spit it out!': Hakuin, *Zen Words for the Heart*, pp. 50–51. 「苦屈苦屈若見一法可依怙驀地須吐却」

p. 186 'It is really . . . a pair of legs': ibid. 「只恨畫蛇添雙脚」

p. 187 'I have come back . . . flexibility of heart': Dogen, *Eiheikoroku*. 「空手にして郷に還る。所以に一毫も仏法無し。」「唯少く柔軟心を得たり。」

p. 187 'Practice then . . . "It is nothing to me" ': Epictetus, *Enchiridion*, ch. I, quoted in https://en.wikipedia.org/wiki/Epictetus.

p. 188 *'I* didn't give up . . . let them go': David Kidd, *Peking Story: The Last Days of Old China* (New York: Clarkson N. Potter, 1988), p. 186.

p. 190 'In the shade . . . dust won't move!': Nakahara Nantenbo (1868–1912), calligraphy scroll. 「竹蔭拂偕塵不動」

Part 8: Attain Supreme, Perfect Enlightenment

p. 198 'Path of No More Learning': Lopez Jr, *The Heart Sutra Explained*, p. 132.

p. 201 'the ability . . . understand both sides': Thich Nhat Hanh, *The Heart of the Buddha's Teaching: Transforming Suffering into Peace, Joy, and Liberation* (New York: Harmony Books, 1998), p. 174.

p. 201 'One may . . . by living': Henry David Thoreau, *Walden* (London: Everyman, 1972), p. 6.

p. 202 'Ignorance and worldly cares . . . unending': Shinran, *Ichinen tanen mon'i* (1256), quoted in http://labo.wikidharma.org/ index.php/一念多念証文.「無明煩悩われらが身にみちみちて、欲もおほく、いかり、はらだち、そねみ、ねたむこころおほくひまなくして、臨終の一念にいたるまでとどまらず、きえず、たえず。」

p. 202 'In this age . . . achieved any of it!': Honen, *Senchaku hongan nenbutsushu* (1198), quoted in http://labo.wikidharma.org/ index.php/選択本願念仏集.「我が末法の時の中の億億の衆生、行を起し道を修せんに、 未だ一人も得る者有らず」

p. 210 'My whole being . . . "Chin Ten Ton"': Dogen, *Shobogenzo: The Treasure House of the Eye of the True Teaching: A Trainee's Translation of Great Master Dogen's Spiritual Masterpiece*, trans. Hubert Nearman (Mount Shasta, CA: Shasta Abbey Press, 2007), p. 28. 「渾身似口掛 空、不問東西南北風、一等爲他談般若。滴丁東了滴丁東。」

Part 9: The Mantra of Great Mystery

p. 215 'Mantras are . . . people can know': Dreitlein (trans.), 'Kūkai's Secret Key to the Heart Sūtra', p. 39. 「已上密說般若。此五種不翻之一也。蓋呪是佛之密語。非下凡所知。」

p. 215 'The quintessence . . . this mantra': Gungthang, quoted in Lopez Jr, *The Heart Sutra Explained*, p. 132.

p. 216 'if M. de Charlus . . . turn the stomach': Marcel Proust, *In Search of Lost Time*, trans. T. Martin, C. K. Scott Moncrieff and A. Mayor, rev. D. J. Enright, 6 vols, e-book edn (New York: Modern Library, 1992), vol. 4: *Sodom and Gomorrah*, p. 599.

p. 219 'In my moment . . . this treasure': Takenaka Tomoyasu, 'Hannya shingyo bekken – sharishi-ko', *Rinzai-shu Myoshinji-ha kyogaku kenkyu kiyo* (May 2004), p. 151, quoting from Xuan-zang's memoirs *Daito jionji sanzohoshi-den* (AD 688). 「危きに在って済はるるを穫たるは寶にこれに憑る所なり。」

p. 219 'It is said . . . Hannya Haramita': ibid., p. 150, quoting from Japanese annals *Zoku nihongi* (AD 797). 「"四句の偈等を受持読誦せば福徳聚まることを得て思い量るべからず"ときく。 . . . 起座行歩に口に閑ひて、皆尽く摩訶般若波羅蜜多を念誦せしむべし。」

p. 220 'All is possible . . . be possible': Nagarjuna, *Vigrahavyavartani* ('Dispeller of Disputes'; second century AD), verse 71.

p. 220 'the uncontrolled element in life': Benoit Mandelbrot, quoted in https://en.wikipedia.org/wiki/Benoit_Mandelbrot.

p. 223 'Within a single sound . . . inexhaustible treasury': Dreitlein (trans.), 'Kūkai's *Secret Key to the Heart Sūtra*', p. 11. 「於一聲中攝藏無量功德。故名無盡藏。」

p. 224 According to Kazuaki Tanahashi . . . knowledge, philosophy, science: Tanahashi, *The Heart Sutra*, p. 196.

p. 224 'Within a moment's reflection . . . a thousand years': Han-shan Deqing, *A Straight Talk on the Heart Sutra*, ed. and trans. Lu K'uan Yü, in *Ch'an and Zen Teaching* (Berkeley, CA: Shambala, 1960), p. 220. 「一念熏修。生死情关忽然隳裂。正如千年暗室。一灯能破。」

p. 228 'Revealed and hidden . . . multilayered': Dreitlein (trans.), 'Kūkai's *Secret Key to the Heart Sūtra*', p. 42. 「顯密在人聲字即非。然猶顯中之祕祕中極祕。淺深重重耳。」

p. 228 'In the eyes . . . he sees gemstones': ibid., p. 41. 「醫王之目觸途皆藥。解寶之人礦石見寶。知與不知何誰罪過。」

p. 229 'abnormality in religious symbology': D. T. Suzuki, quoted in 'Why is There a Dhāraṇī in the Heart Sūtra?', *Jayarava's Raves* website, 18 October 2013 (http://jayarava.blogspot.com/2013/10/why-is-there-dharani-in-heart-sutra.html).

p. 229 'apparently a degradation . . . unintelligible': D. T. Suzuki, *Essays in Zen Buddhism*, Third Series (London: Rider and Company, 1934), p. 217.

p. 229 'What is the meaning . . . so to speak?': ibid., p. 210.

p. 229 'Cherish the great mantra of your own nature': Hakuin, *Zen Words for the Heart*, p. 34. 「可貴自性大神呪」

p. 230 'The mind which cherishes . . . bodhisattva's practice': Dalai Lama, quoted in Barbara O'Brien, 'Bodhicitta: Practice for the Benefit of All Beings', *Learn Religions* website (https://www.learnreligions.com/teachings-about-bodhicitta-450009, updated 28 October 2019).

p. 230 'The Bodhisattva aims . . . no sentient beings': Nagarjuna, quoted in Brunnhölzl, *The Heart Attack Sutra*, p. 47.

p. 231 'Whenever in the course of my life . . . true goodness': Proust, *In Search of Lost Time*, trans. Martin et al., vol. 1: *Swann's Way*, p. 89.

p. 232 '*Hannya* is like a sword . . . not the ignorant!': Hanshan Deqing, *A Straight Talk on the Heart Sutra*, p. 220. 「般若如宵練。遇物即斷。物斷而不自知。非神聖者不能用。況小丈夫哉。」

Part 10: The Chant

p. 236 'It has already . . . achieve victory': Hanshan Deqing, *A Straight Talk on the Heart Sutra*, p. 219. 「然既曰般若。而又名

咒者。何也。极言神效之速耳。如軍中之密令。能默然奉行者。
无不決勝。」

p. 240 'Each letter . . . holds infinite truths': Dreitlein, 'Kūkai's *Secret Key to the Heart Sūtra*', p. 9. 「一字中含無邊義。一點內吞塵數理。」

p. 240 'Inscribed with the brush . . . the sutra book': ibid., p. 9. 「山毫點溟墨 乾坤經籍箱。」

p. 243 'It keeps talking . . . twittering swallows?': Hakuin, *Zen Words for the Heart*, pp. 83–4. 「第二重亦在。漁唱薪歌著何處、鷺吟燕語作麼生？」

p. 246 Fazang, with his eye for detail . . . help others: Fazang, *Hannya shingyo rakuso*, p. 186. 「重言羯諦者、自度度他也。」

p. 246 'the last line . . . usually not translatable': Sheng Yen, *There is No Suffering: A Commentary on the Heart Sutra* (Elmhurst, NY: Dharma Drum Publications, 2001), p. 115.

p. 248 Another version . . . single sound *Om*: Ji Yun, 'Is the Heart Sūtra an Apocryphal Text? A Re-examination', trans. Chin Shih-Foong (8 March 2018), p. 22 (https://www.academia.edu/36116007/Is_the_Heart_Sūtra_an_Apoc-ryphal_Text_A_Re-examination). 「一字般若波羅蜜多経」

p. 250 'Utterly exhausted . . . mantra of the *Prajnaparamita*': Suzuki, *Essays in Zen Buddhism*, p. 216.

p. 252 'blessings to': Tanahashi, *The Heart Sutra*, p. 204.

p. 252 '*Sowaka* . . . fast as possible': Fazang, *Hannya shingyo rakuso*, p. 185.「言薩婆訶者。此云速疾也。謂欲令前所作速疾成就故云爾。」

p. 253 'As the Blessed One . . . had said': Tenzin Gyatso, *Essence of the Heart Sutra*, p. 61.

p. 253 'After reciting this mantra . . . waves of blessing': Jamyang Gawai Lodrö, *Thorough Elucidation of the Meaning of the Words: An Exposition of the Heart of Wisdom*, quoted in ibid., p. 161.

Acknowledgements

As this book took shape over several years, my friends gave countless hours as I read newly written segments to them in the kitchen, or over the phone. Other friends accepted the heavier task of checking the manuscript, even though most of them had never heard of, nor had any particular interest in, the Heart Sutra.

One who did know the Heart Sutra well was Shea Ingram, old friend and scholar of Chinese Buddhism, who saved me from some grievous errors. Other listeners, readers and people who helped along the way were: Sky Alderson, Diane Barraclough, Paul Cato, Ingrid Dankmeyer, Gary DeCoker, Elia De Matteis, John Holden, Thomas Kerr, Ronnarong Khampha ("Ong"), Jonathan Krauth, Felix Krienke, David McAllister, Sam and Jacob Mortimer, Alexandra Munroe, Atsuyuki Ohshima, Timo Ojanen, Tanachanan Phetchsombat ("Saa") Abbas Rasul, Vitsanu ('Soe') Riewseng, Gwen Robinson, Peter Shrieve-Don, Kathy Arlyn Sokol, Charles Tharp, Timothy Toohey and Geoffrey Yu.

To all of them, and the masters of past and present on whose work this rests, I offer my deep gratitude.

ALLEN LANE
an imprint of
PENGUIN BOOKS

Also Published

Lisa Miller, *The Awakened Brain: The Psychology of Spirituality and Our Search for Meaning*

Michael Pye, *Antwerp: The Glory Years*

Christopher Clark, *Prisoners of Time: Prussians, Germans and Other Humans*

Rupa Marya and Raj Patel, *Inflamed: Deep Medicine and the Anatomy of Injustice*

Richard Zenith, *Pessoa: An Experimental Life*

Michael Pollan, *This Is Your Mind On Plants: Opium—Caffeine—Mescaline*

Amartya Sen, *Home in the World: A Memoir*

Jan-Werner Müller, *Democracy Rules*

Robin DiAngelo, *Nice Racism: How Progressive White People Perpetuate Racial Harm*

Rosemary Hill, *Time's Witness: History in the Age of Romanticism*

Lawrence Wright, *The Plague Year: America in the Time of Covid*

Adrian Wooldridge, *The Aristocracy of Talent: How Meritocracy Made the Modern World*

Julian Hoppit, *The Dreadful Monster and its Poor Relations: Taxing, Spending and the United Kingdom, 1707-2021*

Jordan Ellenberg, *Shape: The Hidden Geometry of Absolutely Everything*

Duncan Campbell-Smith, *Crossing Continents: A History of Standard Chartered Bank*

Jemma Wadham, *Ice Rivers*

Niall Ferguson, *Doom: The Politics of Catastrophe*

Michael Lewis, *The Premonition: A Pandemic Story*

Chiara Marletto, *The Science of Can and Can't: A Physicist's Journey Through the Land of Counterfactuals*

Suzanne Simard, *Finding the Mother Tree: Uncovering the Wisdom and Intelligence of the Forest*

Giles Fraser, *Chosen: Lost and Found between Christianity and Judaism*

Malcolm Gladwell, *The Bomber Mafia: A Story Set in War*

Kate Darling, *The New Breed: How to Think About Robots*

Serhii Plokhy, *Nuclear Folly: A New History of the Cuban Missile Crisis*

Sean McMeekin, *Stalin's War*

Michio Kaku, *The God Equation: The Quest for a Theory of Everything*

Michael Barber, *Accomplishment: How to Achieve Ambitious and Challenging Things*

Charles Townshend, *The Partition: Ireland Divided, 1885-1925*

Hanif Abdurraqib, *A Little Devil in America: In Priase of Black Performance*

Carlo Rovelli, *Helgoland*

Herman Pontzer, *Burn: The Misunderstood Science of Metabolism*

Jordan B. Peterson, *Beyond Order: 12 More Rules for Life*

Bill Gates, *How to Avoid a Climate Disaster: The Solutions We Have and the Breakthroughs We Need*

Kehinde Andrews, *The New Age of Empire: How Racism and Colonialism Still Rule the World*

Veronica O'Keane, *The Rag and Bone Shop: How We Make Memories and Memories Make Us*

Robert Tombs, *This Sovereign Isle: Britain In and Out of Europe*

Mariana Mazzucato, *Mission Economy: A Moonshot Guide to Changing Capitalism*

Frank Wilczek, *Fundamentals: Ten Keys to Reality*

Milo Beckman, *Math Without Numbers*

John Sellars, *The Fourfold Remedy: Epicurus and the Art of Happiness*

T. G. Otte, *Statesman of Europe: A Life of Sir Edward Grey*

Alex Kerr, *Finding the Heart Sutra: Guided by a Magician, an Art Collector and Buddhist Sages from Tibet to Japan*

Edwin Gale, *The Species That Changed Itself: How Prosperity Reshaped Humanity*

Simon Baron-Cohen, *The Pattern Seekers: A New Theory of Human Invention*

Christopher Harding, *The Japanese: A History of Twenty Lives*

Carlo Rovelli, *There Are Places in the World Where Rules Are Less Important Than Kindness*

Ritchie Robertson, *The Enlightenment: The Pursuit of Happiness 1680-1790*

Ivan Krastev, *Is It Tomorrow Yet?: Paradoxes of the Pandemic*

Tim Harper, *Underground Asia: Global Revolutionaries and the Assault on Empire*

John Gray, *Feline Philosophy: Cats and the Meaning of Life*

Priya Satia, *Time's Monster: History, Conscience and Britain's Empire*

Fareed Zakaria, *Ten Lessons for a Post-Pandemic World*